Have
Heart,
Will
Travel

Have Heart, Will Travel

Personal Experiences and Practical Guidelines
for Volunteer Mission Trips

Jeannine K. Carter

Jeannine K Carter

PROVIDENCE HOUSE PUBLISHERS
Franklin, Tennessee

Scripture taken from the KING JAMES VERSION except for a reference in the foreword from the HOLY BIBLE, NEW INTERNATIONAL VERSION. Copyright © 1973, 1978, 1984 International Bible Society. Used by permission of Zondervan Bible Publishers.

Printed in the United States of America

01   00   99   98   97   5   4   3   2   1

Library of Congress Catalog Card Number: 96–71626

ISBN: 1–57736–024–9

Photographs provided courtesy of Jeannine K. Carter. Several come from postcards and other materials collected by Carter in her world travels. Illustrations on pages 35, 42, and 43 by Elaine Kernea. Cover by Bozeman Design.

PROVIDENCE HOUSE PUBLISHERS
238 Seaboard Lane • Franklin, Tennessee 37067
800-321-5692

To my many faithful prayer partners who have prayed for me before, during, and after my mission trips. Their prayers have been the real key to the blessings I have received. Just as if they had been on the mission fields with me, these prayer partners have truly had a part in helping persons in many countries to become new Christians.

Contents

Forewords

FOR ANYONE WHO HAS EVER BEEN ON A PARTNERSHIP mission trip, this book is like vicariously experiencing it all over again. For anyone who has yet to taste that thrilling adventure, here is your own personal, practical, exciting guidebook on what to expect and how to prepare. You can watch God at work. Reading these pages makes me ready to go again—right now!

—LARRY WALKER
Ambassador at Large
First Baptist Church, Dallas, Texas

ALL SERIOUS AND THOUGHTFUL CHRISTIANS ARE aware of the last and Great Commission of Jesus to the church: "Therefore go and make disciples of all nations, baptizing them in the name of the Father and of the Son and of the Holy Spirit, and teaching them to obey everything I have commanded you" (Matt. 28:20 NIV). For nearly two millennia, Christians have carried this out, particularly since the onset of the so-called "modern missionary movement" about two hundred years ago.

In recent years, however, a significant change has taken place in how and by whom the task of worldwide evangelization is being undertaken. Alongside career missionaries, who spend years and sometimes lifetimes serving Christ in the places of their calling, have arisen multiplied thousands of part-timers—men, women, and youth—who serve for a few days or a few weeks in a concerted, highly focused outreach to a carefully chosen area. Sometimes, this is done as part of denominational strategy, sometimes with para-church ministries, and sometimes on a freelance basis by an individual or group prompted by the Spirit to take some bold initiative.

Those of us who have participated in such programs can testify to their effectiveness when they are carefully planned and backed by intensive prayer. They bring the Good News to the lost, hope and encouragement to national host pastors and churches, and immeasurable satisfaction and spiritual renewal to the participants. Only God knows the cumulative impact for the kingdom that these efforts have achieved.

Some are able or willing to do such a thing once in a lifetime. Others, however, become so infected by the challenge and opportunity that they become almost full-time part-timers. This is an apt description of Jeannine Carter. For well over a decade, she has gone literally around the world sharing the gospel and using her considerable talents in every situation imaginable. As her Sunday School teacher for many years, I heard her testify again and again to the transforming power of the gospel as God used her and her comrades in Brazil, Mexico, India, South America, Eastern Europe, and the Far East. Though the message and often the methods were the same, the circumstances were unique in each place and time and thus, each account she related was a brand new story of God's faithfulness.

Because Jeannine kept such detailed journals for each trip, she was able to bring the adventure to her audience in vivid, unforgettable ways. Many of her friends would ask if she had any plans to put her notes into a more systematic, comprehensive form so they could understand even better what was involved in this kind of ministry. Now, at last, she has done this in the form of this remarkable book. Year by year, trip by trip, *SHE SHARES HER HEART FOR GOD AND FOR MISSIONS* in ways that compel the reader to go with her and to partake of the excitement, fear, passion, joy, satisfaction, and the thousand and one other emotions that attend doing the will of God in unfamiliar places.

I have known Jeannine and her loving and supportive husband Jim for many years. Therefore, I am in a position to know that the Jeannine of this book is the same Jeannine of everyday life—committed, caring, visionary, indefatigable, and unswerving in obedient faith. Short of going with her on the adventures she describes—a daunting challenge for most of us—this book takes the reader instead both to the ends of the earth and deep into the heart of a woman who loves Jesus and the world he came to save.

—EUGENE H. MERRILL
Professor of Old Testament Studies
Dallas Theological Seminary, Dallas, Texas

Preface and Acknowledgments

WORLD TRAVELER! THAT TITLE HAS BECOME MY nickname in recent years. However, a title that means far more to me, and one that best describes me, is missionary—not a career missionary but a lay missionary. The purpose of this book is to share the experiences that the Lord has given me during the past fifteen years and to encourage you to allow the Lord to give you a heart for missions, convincing you that "If God could use Jeannine, he can surely use me."

It is important for you to know that God had to truly work a miracle in my life (and you will read of several miracles throughout the book) to get me to the point of even considering a mission trip. I have always been an introvert. When I lived overseas in Germany with my husband, Jim, I would never have thought of venturing out of town alone. Many military wives would take American Express tours when their husbands would be gone for weeks at a time. But those adventures were not for me. I feared not understanding the currency exchange, eating strange cuisine, and getting sick without having access to doctors from the United States. I enjoyed the American way of life with Americans.

I first thought of a mission trip in the summer of 1980 when my church (First Baptist Church, Dallas, Texas) made the decision to participate in Texas Baptists' partnership mission endeavor with Brazil in 1981. Texas's largest cities were teamed with Brazil's largest cities. Houston (Texas's largest city) was in partnership with Sao Paulo (Brazil's largest city). Dallas (Texas's second largest city) became a partner with Rio de Janeiro (Brazil's second largest city). Many of us were overwhelmed by the needs presented and the opportunities available.

Soon, my thoughts turned to financing the trip. I had worked the previous year as a substitute teacher to make enough money for our son Jimmie to go with the Chapel Choir (our church teen choir) to Israel. So, I felt reasonably sure, I could try one more year to finance my trip to Brazil. My husband was retiring from the military and beginning a new career, so it was not going to be possible for him to go. But the most fantastic miracle was that the Lord simply took away my fear of traveling alone. It honestly never even crossed my mind to worry about money exchange, the food, and other matters. I knew God had given me an assignment and equipped me for the task. All I needed to do was to be obedient; God is interested in our availability, not our ability.

Being an introvert, I am uneasy about speaking to groups of people. If anyone had ever told me years ago that I would be sharing my testimony before high school student bodies in Africa and Australia, defending myself before customs officials in Mainland China, and coping with numerous other ordeals, I would have shaken my head in disbelief. But I say to you today, God is faithful and prepares you for his service. When I return from mission trips, my most difficult task is to share with groups what the Lord has done. Deep down, I want to do it, but it is a struggle. Even in January I have been known to sweat through a suit jacket while speaking. I tend to be a very private person, not sharing many intimate thoughts.

For several years many people have suggested to me that I should write a book. I have brushed them off, even though I have had some comical experiences as well as the privilege of personally seeing and working on every continent (excluding Antarctica); and I laughingly would reply, "Perhaps if I'm bored with retirement someday and have nothing else to do." However, I can look back now and reply, "It was not God's time," because on my trip to China in 1995, God unmistakably laid it on my heart to write this book. I cannot believe the enthusiasm he has given me for the project. I have only two goals. I want to share how God has used one individual and the blessings that have been mine, and most importantly, I pray that the Lord will touch your heart and life and call you out to serve him in partnership mission work.

A missionary has been defined as "God's person in God's place doing God's work in God's way for God's glory."[1] Shouldn't that describe each of us?

I wish to thank my sister, Kay Breault, for word processing my manuscript. This was no small feat, for I am not known for legible handwriting.

I would also like to thank the following organizations: International Crusades, Michael Gott Evangelistic Association, Campus Crusade for Christ, and World Help. These organizations have given me opportunities to follow Christ's Great Commission to the ends of the earth.

NOTE

1. Millie Stamm, *Meditation Moments* (Grand Rapids: Zondervan, 1967), March 15 entry.

Have
Heart,
Will
Travel

1
Speaking Through an Interpreter

Brazil 1981

M Y PREPARATION FOR THIS TRIP BEGAN MANY months prior to departure. Libby Daniels, the median adult director for our church, First Baptist, Dallas, Texas, was the coordinator. I could not have had better training for all future trips. I have shared many times information gleaned from that orientation. She taught us the culture of the country and how it differed from America. For example, we never made a circle with our thumb and index finger to illustrate A-OK. In Brazil, that is an obscene gesture. We practiced touching the cheek of another on each side to greet someone instead of extending the American handshake.

We were blessed with a Brazilian lady who taught us some Portuguese phrases. Many times, I am asked if I speak the language of each country to which I have gone. The answer is a resounding no. There is no way I could learn all those languages. For most trips, interpreters are provided. More than once, however, I have led people to Christ without an interpreter. The Holy Spirit is the best interpreter we can have, so never think you must be a linguist to be effective on the mission field. It is great to know some key phrases because nationals appreciate it when Americans make an effort to say "good morning" in their native tongue. By the way, it helps to know the word for rest room.

Another serious item to remember: In the United States it is so common to say flippantly, "Come see me sometime." We may or may not intend for the person to take us seriously. Let me give you a word of caution. Do not ever say that in a foreign country unless you truly mean it. You may have many guests. There are true stories about a person showing up on the doorstep of a "flippant inviter" with no advance notice and staying six months at the home. This could be a touchy situation. It could hurt the Christian case and cause angry and hurt feelings for the national and perhaps a new Christian. One Baptist pastor from the United States extended an invitation to provide room and board for a Baptist pastor's daughter in another country to study one year in America, and the agreement resulted in a four-year stay; and now another child has arrived to study (for four years?).

Along this same line, do not ever promise to send money after you return if it is not your intention to do so. You will observe so much need in so many places, and it is easy to get caught up in the emotion of the moment and promise the moon to your new friends. Many times, they or their churches will be devastated by your failure to follow through with your commitment.

Another emphasis during orientation was the exchange of money. Always use a reputable exchange. In most countries, you will find people on the street most happy to give you a better rate of exchange. That is the black market. Do not participate unless you want to see what a foreign jail looks like. One American was arrested and taken to jail for such a transaction. Often, a local bank gives a better rate than a hotel. Coordinators usually have up-to-date information regarding rates. A calculator is a must to determine what you have in U.S. currency versus foreign currency. Please do not ask a national how much something is in "real money." His money is as real to him as yours is to you. "Funny money" isn't a favorite term either. I recommend writing the amount in American dollars when you use a charge card overseas. I got ripped off in Rome. When the charge came through on MasterCard, it was about fifty dollars more than it was supposed to be. In China, one clerk really got hostile and told me I could not use my charge card.

We were given pointers regarding interacting with interpreters. These proved to be helpful suggestions.

- Use short sentences and phrases, and speak slowly and clearly. Pause often to give time for the translator. There is some advantage in having the same interpreter during the time you are there, if it can be arranged. (If a demonstration can take place during one of the group orientation sessions before you go, you will get a good idea of what it is like to speak through an interpreter.)
- Jokes usually will not translate. It is best not to try to use them without first checking them out with your interpreter.
- Poems and hymns will not translate. Flowery language will also make it difficult for your interpreter.
- Do not use idiomatic sayings (i.e., "out on a limb," "shot in the arm").
- Be prepared to help with the cost of some meals and perhaps a small honorarium for interpreters. Your group leader should handle this.
- Give to the interpreter in advance all Bible passages you plan to use.
- Provide the interpreter with an outline of your message in advance.
- Remember, you have half as long to say what you need to say. To give a five-minute testimony, you speak only two and a half minutes, allowing another two and a half minutes for the translation.
- Do not talk about your interpreter. He/she will find it most difficult to talk about self.
- You need not read a Scripture text in English; let the interpreter read it in his/her language.
- Always take a few minutes to pray together before the service begins.
- It would be a courtesy not to ask your interpreter questions all day long. Use the person only when needed. Use what native

language you know to order food and to care for other basic
matters. Remember, you have the tools to witness without an
interpreter.

- Do not talk about your state or the United States in a bragging
  way. When you are asked about your state or the United
  States, do not compare either to their country. Sincerely
  compliment listeners on their country.

- When needed, ask an interpreter to translate from his/her
  language to English for the others in your group (as in inviting
  listeners to accept Christ as Savior).

As you can see, I felt I was very well prepared for my first
adventure. The day of departure came. Over one hundred from the
church were obedient to God's call. We were divided into twenty
teams going to twenty different churches in the Rio area. My
church was in Jacarepagua, a small suburb forty-five minutes from
Rio. In orientation we were told to be flexible—to allow God to use
us as he saw fit in his infinite wisdom. I also learned God has a
sense of humor. I learned that truth quickly when I was asked to
be the pianist for the general services. At that time, my piano
expertise was playing for five year olds in Sunday School. Who
should be leading the music for the revival but a professor of
music from the Baptist seminary in Rio. This, of course, gave me
great confidence. Seriously, he did a great job of covering up my
mistakes. I learned again the age-old truth—God will never ask us
to do anything that he will not equip us to do. Again—it is not our
ability, but our availability.

Even my availability was hindered for several days. After I
gave my testimony and stepped off the podium on the second day
of the crusade, the step slid out from under me and sent me to the
floor. What an embarrassing moment! I sustained a sprained ankle
and hobbled for three or four days. I later introduced plastic shoes
to Dallas since "jellies" (as they were called in Brazil) were all I
could wear. Style was not the Brazilian priority either. Plastic shoes
went with Sunday clothes like tennis shoes would.

Another area where flexibility came to be appreciated was
time. Brazil is much like Mexico. You never get in a hurry (except

when driving). The church service might be scheduled for 7:00 P.M. but would begin about 8:00. This was a truth that I was thankful to learn on my first trip because many other countries operate on the same premise. Even though I am a firm believer in beginning and ending on time, I learned to adapt to the "lazy faire" timetable. We Americans had to keep reminding each other that we were on "Brazilian time," not American time.

Earlier, I mentioned driving. My husband loves for me to go on mission trips. When I return, I usually do not gasp or say much about his driving for a month after I return. His wild driving cannot match the drivers in Rio, Mexico City, or India.

Our group experienced another culture shock very quickly. We were eating on the balcony of a restaurant outdoors soon after we arrived. We witnessed an accident on the street below between a car and a pedestrian. The pedestrian was killed. Someone just walked out into the street, picked up the body, and threw it on the curb; others simply went about their business. Some put no value on human lives, people for whom Christ died.

While in Brazil we toured the Baptist seminary, the publishing house, the Woman's Missionary Union office, and a school. It is always a privilege to meet our Southern Baptist missionaries and encourage them in their ministries. We went sightseeing at Copacabana Beach, Sugar Loaf Mountain, and Corcovado Mountain. (The statue "Christ the Redeemer" on Corcovado Mountain weighs 1,145 tons. The statue of Christ at Eureka Springs, Arkansas, is a replica of this one.) Rio is one of the most beautiful cities.

Sightseeing is a controversial topic on mission trips. One school of thought is to avoid all sightseeing and touring. Those supporting such an attitude say, "We're here only to witness." The mission trips are very expensive. I believe in being a good steward of the Lord's money; I also believe he wants us to enjoy his handiwork. However, when he gives me the resources to make a trip, I want to see everything possible. The chances of ever returning to that same location are slim to none. It is absolutely breathtaking to view God's handiwork at Sugar Loaf Mountain.

Saying good-bye is one of the hardest and saddest experiences on every mission trip. Occasionally, upon arrival, some people keep their distance. As you leave, you weep because of the distance. You have worked alongside such dedicated Christian people, eaten in their homes, and stood beside them as they have seen family members come to Christ. You have seen strangers on the street walk away from you with a lift in their step and a smile on their face since they have given their hearts to Jesus Christ, perhaps from a background of spiritism which is very prevalent in Brazil. You stand in awe, tears streaming down your face (and I do not cry easily), as the Brazilians wave handkerchiefs at you as your bus departs for the airport; you realize you may never see them again this side of eternity—but you realize heaven will be more precious because of your new friends in South America.

2

Sharing Christ in Lay Witness

Brazil 1982

I N 1982 OUR CHURCH COMMITTED AGAIN TO THE TEXAS Baptist partnership with Brazil. I did not attend any of the preparation this time. About three weeks prior to departure, Libby Daniels, the coordinator for the trip, approached me at church. She asked, "Why are you not going to Brazil this year?" I explained what a wonderful and inspirational trip I had had the year before. I have found from my experience that when you go back to a place, it is never the same and is usually a disappointment. I did not want anything to put a damper on my wonderful memories. She commented, "Jeannine, I had the same attitude at the beginning. But as I prayed, the Lord gave me this thought. When one thinks that way, you are limiting God. You're saying he cannot give you as great an experience as the first time. Please pray about going again." That same night, we observed the Lord's Supper. I was sitting in church partaking of it, praying about what I had just heard. At that time, the Lord revealed to me that I was to go again to Brazil.

Trip number two was totally different. Our theme song for the first trip had been "Great Is Thy Faithfulness." It was chosen because the Lord had performed many miracles before that trip with some people getting passports, visas, and financial support at the last minute enabling many people to make the trip. The last Sunday night before this trip, we were notified that the evangelist who was supposed to be our preacher for the crusade could not go for health reasons. One way the trip was different was that we were not divided into teams or churches. It was to be one gigantic crusade held in the huge soccer stadium in Rio. The city had publicized it on billboards, television, and in other ways. Now we were without a speaker. As a group, we bowed our heads and knelt, praying for God to give us his preacher. As we arose joining hands to again sing from our hearts "Great Is Thy Faithfulness," we all knew someone would be led to go. That individual was Gil Stricklin of the Baptist Foundation of Texas. God richly blessed Gil's ministry with thousands of souls.

Our testimonies were printed in Portuguese, and we went door to door during the day sharing Christ. Another tool we used was a cardboard design configured to play a record with the plan of salvation heard by rotating the record with a pen. An interpreter would go with us and introduce us. In Brazil, no one has a doorbell. You clap your hands to alert the resident of your presence. My interpreter would introduce me: "Jeannine has come from the United States to share something with you. May we come in?" With no exception, we were invited in. This has been the method I have used on most of my mission trips. It is extremely successful. It is a method used to teach nationals how to witness. It gives them boldness. They see how their own people respond to the gospel. It gives encouragement to the American mission volunteer. I have had the door slammed in my face in my own city and my own block more than once. That has never been my experience on mission trips.

It is exciting to go places where people are eager to hear what God is doing in your life. I have been confronted many times with the question, "Why go to another country to witness? There are enough lost people in America." I agree with that evaluation. However, the Bible tells us to "shake off the very dust from your feet for a testimony against them" (Luke 9:5). We should never give up on our friends, neighbors, coworkers, but I believe God sends many of us to countries where the gospel is being accepted in extraordinary numbers, where people are eager to hear and heed his gospel.

One of the many results of mission trips is the change they bring about in the lives of those who go. We gained a confidence in witnessing we did not have before going. It made us more alert to those around us who may not have known Christ. The Lord has called out many to serve him full-time on the mission field as a result of a two-week trip. Richard Shaffer is a layperson who has served in Brazil since 1986. He has seen over twenty thousand people come to the Lord. The Brent Rays serve as Foreign Mission Board appointees in Brazil. Linda Almond served one year. The Lord has used mission trips to revitalize churches' visitation programs and to serve as an impetus for mission giving. The benefits of the Southern Baptist Lottie Moon Christmas Offering on the mission fields are evident. In Brazil we saw the publishing house built entirely with Lottie Moon money.

The most exciting experience I had on this trip was my encounter with a navy wife. On a door-to-door excursion, I met a lady new to Rio. She was embarrassed about her home full of boxes, having just moved. I immediately related to her our military background. We had instant communication. We shared similar officer wives' experiences. I was able to relay to her the peace that comes in the midst of turmoil through a relationship with Jesus Christ. She was excited about accepting him as her personal Savior. That, folks, was a "divine appointment." I do not believe it was an accident that out of the more than one hundred of us knocking on doors that day (no one else had a military background), I was teamed with her.

It was a joy to work with Nelson Fanini, pastor of First Baptist Church, Niteroi (a suburb of Rio). He is often referred to as the "Billy Graham of Brazil." (Later in the book, you will read that I have also worked with the "Billy Graham of South Africa." I call these opportunities to work with such godly men "icing on the cake.") First Baptist, Niteroi, has a membership of over four thousand with seventy-five other preaching points in the area. The church was founded by W. Bagby, a Baptist missionary from Texas. When Pastor Fanini went there in 1964, there were six hundred members. He has seen phenomenal growth. One hundred and six television channels carry his weekly broadcast. He is currently president of the Baptist World Alliance. Our team was most appreciative of his support and leadership in the crusade.

3

Surviving Taxi Rides and Illness

Brazil 1983

IN 1983, MEMBERS OF FIRST BAPTIST CHURCH, DALLAS, were off to Brazil again. Since the Lord had given me two unique mission trips (and he was blessing my substitute teaching that was funding my trips), I did not hesitate to volunteer the third time around. Again, this was a very different kind of trip. We were asked by First Baptist Church, Niteroi, to conduct Vacation Bible Schools at their main church and their preaching points. We took all the supplies and handiwork with us. On several days, we had 150 children on the side of a mountain; each was eager to hear about Jesus.

One free night, my roommate Birdie Briggs and I decided we would go out for dinner. From the many trips Jim and I have taken, we have learned to eat where the nationals eat. So Birdie and I asked at the hotel desk where a good Brazilian restaurant was located and how long it would take to go there. We proceeded to get into a cab and give the driver the address. It was to be a ten-minute drive. Ten minutes turned into twenty minutes, and twenty minutes turned into thirty minutes. Psalm 56:3, "What time I am afraid, I will trust in thee," became very real to us as we kept looking at each other and silently praying, all the while wondering if we were ever to see our hotel again. (The driving had already

*Slums in Brazil. Courtesy—the*Commission *magazine. Used by permission of the Foreign Mission Board of the Southern Baptist Convention.*

prepared us for our step into eternity.) Finally, we did arrive at a quaint Brazilian home out in the country that had been converted into a cozy typical restaurant. I ordered pepper steak (assuming it to be Chinese pepper steak, since that was all I had ever eaten). It was a real delicacy—no green peppers but black pepper and peppercorns. It was a delicious treat and one we thoroughly enjoyed after we thanked God for his protection. We agreed that the ten minutes quoted for the trip was "ministerially speaking."

I had my first experience of becoming ill on a mission trip. I always follow the directions of the coordinator. We were told not to eat salads or unpeeled fruit. But even following all directions, my turn came. Our plane went through violent weather coming home; I learned how to use an airsickness bag rather quickly. Then someone suggested I take Dramamine; that person did not know how I react to medicine. So, on an empty stomach, I proceeded to take the miracle drug. Let me tell you, I was feeling "very good" by the time we reached Miami. Walking a straight line was out of the question. Going through customs with a "tipsy gait" and slurred speech made one wonder what kind of mission endeavor had been enjoyed. Luckily, our plane to Dallas was late departing, so we had a good American breakfast which helped immensely.

The Mission to Brazil Partnership with Texas has been "the most massive undertaking in the history of partnership evangelism. It involved 3,740 volunteers from Texas in approximately 150 projects; 90,500 professions of faith were recorded, and 57 new churches were established."[1] Nelson Fanini said, "Out of every 10 people you witness to in Brazil, one will not listen to you, five will hear you and thank you, and four will accept Christ as their Lord and Savior." What if we had these statistics in the United States?

NOTE

1. Bill Damon, "Official Report on Brazil-Texas Partnership Mission," 1.

4

Enjoying the Culture of Another Country

Mexico 1984 and 1985

B APTISTS' PARTICIPATION IN THE EVANGELIZATION OF Mexico dates from the early 1800s. Real organization started in 1803 with the National Baptist Convention and the sending of forty missionaries by the Southern Baptist Foreign Mission Board. Much still remains to be done. Less than one half of one percent of the population is Baptist. Beginning in 1985, the convention hoped to name a couple for foreign mission service each year until the year 2000. First Baptist Church, Dallas, joined Texas Baptists in 1984 and 1985 to accept a partnership with Mexico. Our church was teamed up with Bethel Baptist Church in Mexico City. We conducted Vacation Bible Schools for them. The Chapel Choir from our church assisted us. It was a blessing working with such dedicated young people. We had the pleasure of attending their concerts also.

One of the Chapel Choir members had an experience he will not forget. Needless to say, his mom will not soon forget it either, for that member was my son Jimmie. The experience only added one more gray hair among my many. He had a date one night with the pastor's daughter. Little did he know he was supposed to ask her father for permission (according to Mexican Baptists' custom). This caused a real upheaval in the church. It is the custom there to go

The National Palace, an architectural gem and seat of the Mexican government

Air view of the Pyramid of the Sun at the Teotihuacan Archaeological Zone

before the church to ask forgiveness when you have sinned. So the pastor's daughter had to acknowledge their mistake, and Jimmie was asked to write a letter to the church. Needless to say, he now knows that dating a Christian in Mexico is certainly different than in the United States. He did not forget that date for a long time.

I learned on this trip how much the body can endure. Little did I know that this would be only my first lesson. I climbed to the top of the Teotihuacan Pyramid; it was two hundred feet high. Dorothy Williams, who was more than eighty years old, taught us to weave our steps as we climbed. It was a lesson I would remember on many future mission trips. Never say you are too old for a mission trip. I have seen several men and women over eighty make trips. The Lord provides the strength for those he calls.

We enjoyed a Mexican folklore ballet. To me it is "icing on the cake" when I get to experience the real culture of the country in which I am serving. The people with whom you serve are proud of their country and, if you express any interest in the area, they are more than happy to share their customs with you. It develops a bond between you. Some of us even braved a bull fight. In 1984 and 1985 were 84 projects, 2,300 participants, and 8,833 professions of faith recorded during the Texas-Baptist Mexico Partnership.

5
Working Through International Crusades

Italy 1984

A FTER THE THREE TRIPS TO BRAZIL AND TWO TO Mexico City, our church ceased the partnership mission endeavors. On the first trip to Brazil, I met Noreen Williams, a member of our church and employee at International Crusades. In 1984, she asked me to pray about going to Rome, Italy, with International Crusades. International Crusades accepts invitations from overseas Baptists to bring Southern Baptists to conduct church-to-church crusades with their people. By this time, I had truly caught the "mission-trip bug," and I was excited about yet another adventure for the Lord.

Noreen and I took a ten-day trip with Cosmos Bus Tours (very inexpensive) through Europe (England, Germany, Belgium, Austria, and Italy) with two other International Crusade couples before meeting the International Crusade team in Rome. We had many opportunities to share Christ and to acquaint our travel partners with the International Crusade organization. Incidentally, I learned early in this trip that other luggage keys could open my luggage. I became grateful for that knowledge when, on the first day of the trip, I locked my luggage and threw the keys on a desk. They slid off the back and lodged between the desk and wall which were attached. Hotel staff used coat hangers and other

means to try to free my keys—unsuccessfully—while a busload of
angry tourists waited for me. So, learning I would not be locked
out of my luggage for two weeks since I could use someone else's
key to open my luggage gave me some consolation.

International Crusades began the crusade with an opening rally.
All the participating churches came together for a worship service
and prayer time for the crusade. The following day, we visited the
catacombs and Paul's prison. Those were spiritual highlights for
me. Words cannot express what my heart felt as we joined hands
and sung "Amazing Grace" at the spot where Paul was imprisoned
and where he wrote the prison epistles. Visiting the Colosseum
where so many Christians lost their lives was indeed humbling.
You realize the price that has been paid that we might have
Scripture, and the responsibility that is ours to "carry the torch."

That evening, we traveled by train to Trebsacce. Noreen and I
served with Marion and Jim Kilbebec from Port Charlotte, Florida.
One exciting thing about International Crusades trips is that you
meet so many wonderful Christians from all over the United States.
There are usually four to six on a team, so you really get to know
them well. When we arrived, we had no interpreter. That evening,
the four of us prayed for one, realizing how absolutely helpless we
were without one, as well as would be the services starting Sunday
morning. God answered our prayers and we began on time. Our
church met in a space equivalent to a one-car garage.

The pastor lived on the premises, and we were housed in an
area much like a dormitory—one big room with cots. After living
out of suitcases for ten days, Noreen and I had anticipated getting
unpacked and hanging our clothes on hangers. Well so much for
that—we shared the room with numerous women and children.
We soon discovered there was no hot water. Later, we learned
there was hot water downstairs, so we were able to trot down each
evening for our shower. There was no water pressure, but when
the water trickled out, it was warm.

I ate my first rabbit on this trip. I was excited. I had always been
told it tasted like chicken. Was I ever disappointed. It was tough
and had no flavor. We soon learned the reason. We had eaten the
family rabbit, and it was very old.

ITALY, 1984

Trieste

2. Milano-Senago Venezia

3. Torino

Firenze ● 4. Ancona

Pisa

The Italian Gospel Mission has 51 churches in Italy. From June 6 to 7, the International Crusades, with head-quarters in Dallas, Texas, arranged a special evangelistic crusade in 12 of these churches in which 50 Christians from Baptist churches in the USA participated. During the crusade, 953 people made decisions for Christ.

● 1. Roma

San 5.●
Giovanni   Brindisi
Martina 6.●Taranto
Napoli   ○Vico   8.●   7.
                 Equence   Massafra

On this map of Italy, the cities in which our churches participated in the crusade are all marked with numbers from 1 through 12.

Not far from Naples is *Vico Equense* where usually every second year our European Workers' Conferences are held. The next Conference, D. V. will be held in June 1985.

Trebi-
9. Sacce
Paola 10.●

Messina 12.   ● 11. Bovalino
Trapani

Palermo

Catania

The crusade went very slowly. International Crusades makes preliminary trips to train the pastors for a crusade. The organization requires a great deal from participating churches. Operation Andrew cards (of prospects) must be used. The churches must adhere to a strict follow-up program after the crusade. We do not win people to Christ and "drop them." International Crusades does not want to take Americans overseas and have them feel that their money has been wasted. But it seems there will always be one church that does not follow through. Our church had not done anything to prepare for us. Furthermore, they were happy just as they

Ruins of ancient Rome near Mamertine prison.

Ancient Colosseum in Rome

Ancient Appian Way

Jim Kilbebec (left) preaching at Trebisacci Church with Maorillo Paolo interpreting

Trebisacci Church

were. They did not care to grow. But we walked the streets, witnessing each morning and late afternoon, and the Lord allowed me to influence nine decisions for Christ.

The Catholic influence was hard to penetrate. However, our testimonies written in Italian were the key. Each is a powerful tool. No one can argue about what God has done in one's individual life. When you share your personal relationship with Jesus Christ, he rewards. We claim the promise that his Word will not return void: "So shall my Word be that goeth forth out of my mouth: it shall not return unto me void, but it shall accomplish that which I please, and it shall prosper in the thing whereto I sent it" (Isa. 55:11).

When the crusade was over, we took an overnight train to Rome. International Crusades had purchased sleeper car tickets for us, but we were not all together. Noreen and I had settled in our compartment when an Italian man joined us. Noreen kept telling him he was in the wrong compartment, but he was as adamant that he was correct. Noreen saw our coordinator down at the end of the sleeper car and in desperation screamed out, "There's a man

in our compartment." Gene Lake, our coordinator, informed her he had a ticket and would remain. I am convinced that after that night, the passenger wanted nothing to do with "those crazy Americans." Our luggage tumbled down on him about 3:00 A.M.

The next day our team departed for the United States—not our designated departure time, but when the Italian pilot decided he wanted to depart. We sat on the runway two hours after boarding the plane. We were told that was a frequent occurrence. It just so happened I was flying to Amarillo, Texas, where I was meeting Jim and a group of teen leaders spending the night there on our way to Glorieta, New Mexico. There was no allowance made to sit on a runway waiting two hours to depart. We were late arriving at John F. Kennedy in New York and literally had to run to make our flight to Dallas. Airline officials (after going through customs) requested that we just leave our luggage in a corner; they would sort it out. That was not very comforting, but we had no choice if we planned to make the Dallas-bound plane.

Upon arriving in Amarillo and sharing my tale of woe with Jim, he was ready to leave the airport and hope the airline could get the luggage to Albuquerque so we could drive two hours back from Glorieta and pick it up. Somehow, I just had a tinge of hope, so we walked to the luggage pick-up and, would you believe, my luggage was the first off the plane, indicating it had been the last on (another miracle).

Another blessing from the trip occurred several months after I returned home. My mother had not looked upon my trips with much enthusiasm. She felt I should wait until my boys were older. I was asked to speak to a Woman's Missionary Union group who knew Mother and invited her to visit that day. She was so visibly moved by how God had used me in Rome that she confided on the way home, "I'll never again question your mission endeavors. God is using you in a special way." That was September 1984. She went to be with the Lord in May 1985. I am grateful she understood the ministry that the Lord had laid on my heart. I was able to report the work of 13 teams (50 individuals) and 953 decisions.

6

Living in Hotels and Homes of Nationals

South Africa 1985

HAVING BEEN SO IMPRESSED WITH INTERNATIONAL Crusades and the wonderful friends I made on the Rome Crusade, I never hesitated a moment to follow the Lord's leadership to South Africa with International Crusades in September 1985 which was, if you remember, at the very height of the rioting in South Africa. I had many opportunities to witness before I departed. So many people were horrified that I would even think of entering that country then. But I was convinced that the Lord who had called me to go would go before me and protect me. Unfortunately, many Americans failed to really trust God for protection and backed out of the crusade. It really made Americans and Christians look bad in the eyes of the South Africans. There were not enough teams for the churches which had requested them; this limited the amount of ministry we could do.

I had the opportunity to stay in the home of a lovely South African family. I had the pleasure of accompanying them to a wedding while staying in their home. Whenever it is possible, we always stay in the homes. There are positive and negative aspects about staying in homes versus hotels. Staying in homes, you can make lifelong friends. You become part of the culture of the country. You develop a camaraderie with the nationals as you pray for the crusade together. On the other hand, staying in hotels gives you camaraderie with other Christians on the crusade. You meet together for breakfast, pray for the crusade, and share each day's blessings and prayer requests. At one of these hotel meetings, we were praising God for the victories we had experienced. One of our group spoke up and shared his frustration, his failures, and the lack of support and response at his church. We all prayed for a change in the church and breathed a prayer each time the Lord brought him to our remembrance during that day. The next day at breakfast he too had great victories to share with us.

Since there were not enough preachers with us, South African preachers had to assist. At Sterling Baptist Church in East London where I served, I had the honor of working with Cecil Peasley who some consider the "Billy Graham of South Africa." He led us in a prayer seminar each morning which prepared us for the afternoon witnessing.

I learned on this trip that it pays to have a famous name. I was scheduled to speak at a high school during the lunchtime. They forgot to announce it on the public address system, and no one showed up. I asked the coordinator if the students remembered Jimmy Carter. She replied in the affirmative. I said, "Go tell everyone Mrs. Jimmie Carter is here to speak to them." Pretty soon we had a room full to capacity. Some did not believe the announcement, so I presented my military identification card, indicating that I was indeed Mrs. Jimmie Carter. It was fun capitalizing on my name. In speaking to high schools in other countries, I always begin by saying they have a freedom we do not have in America. I cannot stand and give my personal testimony and share Christ in an American high school. That statement usually flabbergasts them.

An exciting postscript to the high school meeting took place. After I returned to the United States, I received a letter from a student who wrote to let me know she accepted Christ several days after the assembly. I still correspond with her and enjoy discipling this student.

The church in East London had no paster, and I admired its members for still participating in the crusade. They were well prepared for us, and God beautifully blessed them.

We had the opportunity to go into nursing homes, schools, hospitals, and the businesses of church members. The music was provided by a Christian music group. The leader had been part of a rock band until he rededicated his life to the Lord, and now he enthusiastically leads Christian music at his church and anywhere else he can get permission to play. They were very popular with all of the high school students, and his testimony reached many students.

After I arrived in South Africa, Cecil Peasley discovered that because of my schedule I would miss the optional trip to Kruger Park, the two-hundred-mile, wild-animal reserve. He said no one should visit South Africa without going on a safari, so he made plans for me to fly in a little four-seater plane to the park. I had never been in that type of plane, and as it wobbled down the runway, I thought my demise was imminent. Never mind the fear I had of the plane not being pressurized for ear comfort. We barely stayed out of the tree limbs. I had a private tour guide and slept in a thatched hut that night, making it back to Johannesburg just in time to board the jet for the United States—another example of "icing on the cake" the Lord has afforded me on all of my mission trips. International Crusades reported 511 decisions with only 32 people and 13 teams participating.

One of the unusual souvenirs I brought back from South Africa was a bust made out of sandstone. It was extremely heavy, and I had to hand carry it.

7

Handling Passports, Food, and Luggage

India 1987

T HE FALL OF 1986 FOUND ME VERY DISAPPOINTED. I had planned to go to Finland. Near the time of departure, Ben Mieth, founder of International Crusades, called to tell me more people had volunteered than could be taken. Many Finnish churches which originally signed up for the crusade had backed out. I had always prayed that if it was not the Lord's will that I go on a certain crusade that he would close the door. He not only closed the door, but he smashed all kinds of plans. My roommate-to-be and I had planned a tour to several other Scandinavian countries. She was selected to go. I had meant my prayer from the bottom of my heart, and I knew that the Lord had answered my prayer. I am so grateful for that "no" because I know the Lord will close the door each time he has better plans for me. That is exciting!

What better plans did God have? In January 1987, I was reading the following article, written by Gary Hearon, from the *Baptist Standard*, our Texas Baptist paper:

Last evening, an informational meeting was held regarding the Partnership Crusade to Hyderabad, India, January 27–February 10, 1987. The meeting was very helpful—challenging and

49

inspiring. Rev. Ben Meith, president of International Crusades and Rev. Calvin Beach, executive vice-president (who has just returned from India) spoke with impassioned plea of the overwhelming need of India for the Lord Jesus and of the magnificent response now being given to the preaching of the Gospel. India is one of the four or five areas of the world where the Spirit of God is moving mightily and literally untold numbers are turning to Christ in repentance and faith. If you were at the recent SBC in Atlanta, you heard Dr. Keith Parks speak to this very thing. India is ripe for the Gospel; the fields are white. . . .

Thirty Baptist churches in Hyderabad—a city of 3 million people (India's fifth largest)—have invited 150 of us to come from Dallas Baptist Association and help them reach their Christless masses. *Will you pray earnestly about going? Will you plan to go unless God closes the door?*

The pastor of the largest Baptist church in Hyderabad (1,200 average attendance) is challenging his people to evangelize and baptize at least 1,000 people as a result of this projected crusade! He is seeking to motivate and inspire other pastors with a similar dream—of doubling their membership/attendance because of these days. May his tribe increase!

God bless you because of your faithful service to Him. Pray with us even now for this crusade and consider the possibility of your going.

It was as if God himself stepped off that page and spoke to me. The part italicized was the "crowning blow." He had closed one door, and I really could not think of a reason not to go. It has been interesting to see how God has used various people, articles, and circumstances to speak to me about crusades. I did not know Gary Hearon. Gary did not know that one weekly article would have such an impact on a life.

Were there ever surprises waiting for me as I prepared for this crusade! Many countries you enter require you to have six months left on your passport. I had checked mine in the fall, and I was safe for the Finland crusade. However, there was not time for India. I had to send mine for a renewal. I would be leaving in less than three weeks. The day before departure, Ben Mieth called and said mine had not arrived. I replied, "Well, I guess I won't be going." He replied, "Jeannine, you do what you think best. But I suggest you go." He explained my passport was to be hand carried to Germany by Lufthansa pilots from Houston (the Texas headquarters for passports). I asked, "What if it doesn't arrive?" "Then, you'll turn around and return because you can't enter Bombay without it."

Immediately, I knew the Lord would not send me to Frankfurt to turn around and come right back, knowing how much I dislike the long transatlantic flights. Seriously, I had seen the Lord work so many miracles with visas and passports on previous trips that it was not difficult for me to ask for a miracle. This situation really bonded our team. Many members of our group came to me during the flight to share that they were praying that my passport would be in Frankfurt when we arrived. This was so reassuring to me.

When we arrived in Frankfurt, before we deplaned, there was an announcement over the public-address system, "Would Jeannine Carter please go to gate fourteen to claim her passport?" Praise the Lord! Another miracle! All the Americans started clapping and rejoicing. The remaining passengers sat stunned. They could not believe it. How did I ever leave the United States without a passport? Why would anyone want to leave without one? Again, as was the case with the South Africa crusade, I had a chance to share my faith and confidence and relationship with Jesus Christ with fellow Americans.

This crusade presented me with another new experience. I had always known my roommate on previous crusades. This time we were strangers. But are we ever really strangers when we are brothers and sisters in Christ? We did have one difference of opinion. Our coordinator had told us before we left that we would not eat any meal outside the hotel. When we arrived, logistics prevented that order from being feasible. The church in Telugu was forty-five minutes away from the hotel. There were two major reasons to avoid that trip three times a day.

First, the drivers are wild beyond comprehension. I just thought the drivers in Rio de Janeiro and Mexico City were reckless. In India, they drive on the wrong side of the road to us Americans. But many times my roommate would whisper, "Look where we are." At those times, we would be on the right side, much to our horror. The taxis are what we called three-wheel buggies with open sides. You remained on the right side with a huge bus coming right at you. When the bumper of your buggy touched the bumper of the bus, the driver swerved quickly to his side of the road. I suppose I have to admit they had some skill because we never crashed, at least not my roommate and I. We soon concluded that food was not worth risking the drive back and forth.

Second, because of the distance, we would spend too much time traveling. So, we ate in the homes of the church members. I only eat enough to be polite. The food was really quite tasty—if you like curry, and I do. Then, what was my problem? We had to walk across open sewage to enter their home. That was where the dishes were washed. While I was playing with my food, my roommate was ravishingly eating every bite and asking for more. This was so embarrassing to me. I made all kinds of excuses. I said my husband did not want a fat wife. I never ate much. After two days, I searched out our coordinator for reassurance. He confirmed that I was correct. It was definitely a time for dieting. (By the way, I did lose fifteen pounds on that crusade. I would definitely recommend mission trips if you have a weight problem.) Seriously, it is so important to follow the coordinator's instructions about food. If you are told to avoid salads, by all means avoid them.

We Americans think we are indestructible sometimes. It is also easy to fall into the trap of feeling that since we are on a mission trip for the Lord, nothing will happen to us. In Brazil, we joked when we were told that our bodies would not be returned to the United States should we meet the Lord while there. (By the way, that is true in many of the countries.) In India, one of our teams had an accident while traveling by taxi. Their driver did not swerve fast enough to miss an oncoming car. They rolled down an embankment but were thrown clear of the vehicle. They escaped with only minor bruises. The Lord really protected them. Our

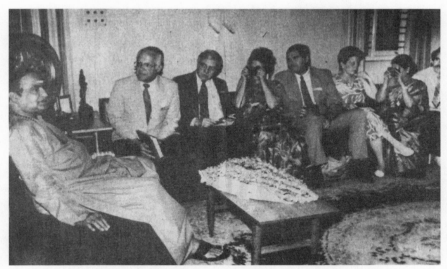

Pastors from USA visited Chief Minister N. T. Rama Rao at his Abids residence

whole group was shaken emotionally. Never again would we presume safety. We must pray for physical protection and good health.

Although I did not know my roommate ahead of time, I did have one traveling companion. My Sunday School class supported an Indian couple attending Dallas Theological Seminary. When my class found out we would be having the crusade near Hyderabad, the Indian wife's hometown, a gift was given, making it possible for her to make the trip. She served as one of our interpreters. It was a blessing for all the Americans to meet the one who had translated all of our testimonies into the various Indian dialects.

We noted that several customs in the churches in India were different from ours. First, everyone takes off his/her shoes when entering. (They could not comprehend the magnanimity of that at my home church. How would one find his/her own shoes in a sea of one thousand pairs? Would one of our megachurches care to imitate such a custom?) The men sit on one side of the church and the women on the other, "and the twain must never meet." The most difficult custom for us was that no invitation was given. Those pastors preach their hearts out and yet never give those present an opportunity to accept Christ.

One night I was given the opportunity to share my personal testimony and to conclude by sharing my thoughts concerning a Christian home. When I sat down and turned the service back to the pastor, he explained I was the "sermon" for the evening. If I was the preacher for the evening, there was no way I was going to pass up that opportunity. I jumped up and gave an invitation, and four people walked down the aisle accepting Christ. Praise the Lord! Not bad for my first sermon. Perhaps I need to change careers! I almost did not live this down when I returned home—our church's first woman preacher! Actually, I broke the ice. The pastor issued an invitation each night for the remainder of the crusade.

Many times the Lord has given me "icing on the cake," as I call special blessings on my trips—weddings, funerals, safaris, special cultural opportunities. While in Hyderabad, I was privileged to accompany Ben Mieth and several Americans to visit the chief minister of Hyderabad. We shared our purpose for coming to India and "planted a seed." Anytime we present the gospel and do not receive a positive response, I call it planting seeds. First Corinthians 3:6–9 reminds us sometimes we merely introduce one to Jesus Christ. Someone following us may see that person actually accept Christ. We are just called to be faithful. His word will not return void. "So shall my Word be that goeth forth out of my mouth: it shall not return unto me void, but it shall accomplish that which I please, and it shall prosper in the thing where to I sent it" (Isa. 55:11).

At a team meeting in our hotel, Ben was sharing with us that we might wonder if all the decisions we were seeing made were for real. Again he reminded us we will never know this side of eternity. We are only called to be faithful and leave the results to God. The next morning, he put me on the spot. In front of everyone, Ben said, "Jeannine, I want to know one thing. Do you think the hotel clerk you witnessed to last night was saved?" Having remembered the previous day's meeting, I replied, "I hope so, I'm leaving the results to the Lord." He said, "I know she was. Would you like to know how I know? This morning she had removed the red dot on her forehead." The red dot signified a Hindu. Presently in India, that is not always true. Indian women use it for makeup like we use rouge. But because it is so closely identified with Hinduism, many remove it when they accept Christ. I thanked God for this unusual proof of a new child of the King.

I had someone designated to assist me with my luggage on the crusade. Before I left for the trip, Jim came home from work with this story. A dedicated Christian who worked for him came to him with a request. His pastor was taking several people to India, and he felt the Lord leading him to make the trip if he could have the time off from work. Naturally, Jim shared that I was going and that, yes, he could go if he assisted me with my luggage. He was only teasing, but I appreciated the assistance. The ability to handle my luggage with no ill effects has been a blessing on every mission trip since I sustained a back injury in an automobile accident many years ago. I must be very careful of what I lift. Many times, I have lifted and dragged luggage to the four corners of this earth that would be a feat for healthy backs. But the Lord has protected me, and not once have I had any problems. The jarring that my back received from the taxis in India dodging potholes in their dirt streets gave me serious concern at the time, but again, God equips us for the tasks he sends us to do. We are the safest when we are in God's perfect plan.

My Indian pastor, in his farewell address to me, quoted Proverbs 25:25: "As cold waters to a thirsty soul, so is good news from a far country." He thanked me for bringing the good news of salvation to them from a far country. Our far country sent 20 teams with 3,298 decisions recorded.

8
Coping With the Unexpected

Australia 1987

NINETEEN EIGHTY-SEVEN FOUND ME "DOWN UNDER" with the Aussies. This trip and my 1985 South African trip were my longest. We flew all night to Frankfurt and then the next night flew all night to Sydney. Again we stayed in homes. The Sloanes were so gracious. They had two adorable girls with whom I fell in love—since I had no girls. They both accepted Christ that week. I am so grateful we experienced instant friendship because later during the week I learned some interesting tidbits of church politics. It appeared the church was not convinced of the merit of a crusade. John Sloane was a church officer and had volunteered his home rather reluctantly to keep a team member. The pastor shared with me the last day that John had recommitted his life during the crusade and had apologized for many unkind remarks made toward the revival effort. This was such a prime example of the Lord putting personalities together.

I always know the coordinators pray concerning which team will go to which church. It is an object of my prayer preparation also. Team members must always be sensitive to the feelings of their host families. A widower in this church had looked forward for months to welcoming Americans into his modest home. He had spent more than his budget would really allow for food and had prepared several casseroles for his special guests. The Americans, upon arrival, surveyed the surroundings, partook of one meal, and promptly told the coordinator they would not stay there, much less eat the horrible food. It created a most embarrassing situation for all concerned and really broke the spirit of the Aussie. Needless to say, such developments could have quenched the Spirit in that crusade.

Fortunately, God is able to move despite the obstacles. My mission trips seem to be mountaintop experiences for me spiritually as I receive such a blessing from the services. As I was blessed by Cecil Peasley in South Africa, Jim and Bettye Webb blessed my heart in Australia. Jim was the evangelist on our team (a pastor from Marble Falls, Texas, at the time, but now he pastors an English-speaking church in Germany). Bettye had a phenomenal testimony of physical healing and a wonderful solo voice which she shared each night. God blessed our services in a miraculous way.

Many Australians are very difficult to reach for the Lord. They are affluent and self-sufficient and feel no need for the Lord—much like Americans. But we witnessed decisions recorded each night. Some were made during the services. Others resulted from our door-to-door encounters during the day or from our visits to senior citizen homes, schools, and hospitals. As we went sight-seeing to Bunya Park (to see kangaroos, koala bears, and other sights) or to the Baptist Retreat Center or to sugar and pineapple plantations, we were cognizant of our opportunities to witness to all whom we met at each sight.

I always take advantage of any optional trips the organization offers. This time we were able to stay for three days in Sydney. We visited the Rocks (Australia's birthplace), the famous Opera House, Old Sydney Town (much like our Jamestown), and took a harbor cruise. We witnessed a sheep-shearing exhibition and an Australian music show. Our written testimonies were adequately distributed throughout Brisbane and Sydney with 344 recorded decisions (9 teams) before all Americans departed gaining back the day we lost traveling to Australia when we crossed the International Date Line. "G' Day, Mate."

Sydney

When I landed in Los Angeles, I knew I was on my own. Juanita, Jim's aunt in San Francisco, had planned to meet me, and we were to tour Los Angeles. She could not get away. I tried to change my ticket and fly home. Because of group rates, I could not do that. So I determined to make the best of my situation and see Los Angeles. I had been told by the passenger next to me on the plane from Sydney that there was an inexpensive but nice motel near the airport. I called the tourist bureau and learned it was closed. I guess I gave the impression I preferred a less expensive motel, so they recommended one. (By the way, I am a frugal person.) The motel's appeal left a lot to be desired, but I registered and went to my room. I soon learned I was not alone in my room. There were many critters, namely roaches. But having been to India earlier, I thought I could handle it one night.

Not wanting to waste any more time, I took a cab to Universal Studios. Finishing my tour, I tried to find a cab to return to my upscale motel. There was not one. I asked a Delta representative at his booth to call for one. He solemnly asked, "Are you alone?" I replied, "Yes." He admonished me not to get a cab there because cabs were not trustworthy. Great! How would I get back to my humble abode? "Catch a shuttle bus to Sheraton and go by cab from there" was his reply. So I jumped on a shuttle bus and proceeded to get off where everyone exited. To this day, I do not know where everyone was headed, but when I got off, I saw the Sheraton sign about a mile up a mountain. It was dark by then. I took off running. At this point, I was thankful that mission trips get you in shape. Needless to say, I had my daily exercise by the time I returned to "Roach Haven."

The next day, I planned to go to Anaheim to Disneyland and just spend the night there. I had to scrap those plans—tourist season! Not a room to be had! So I rode the bus down and then back. However, I dragged all my luggage one block to another motel, leaving all the critters behind. The next day, I headed for the airport, but was initiated into a typical Los Angeles traffic jam. Everyone else on the shuttle bus missed his/her flight, but this seasoned traveler had allowed sufficient time for such eventualities. I sat by a Los Angeles citizen on the plane who sheepishly shared with me that I had resided on the edge of the red-light district. The Lord does take care of naive, unsuspecting tourists in Los Angeles.

When Jim and I finally drove up our driveway, he turned to me and asked, "Did anything happen in Australia? All I've heard about is Los Angeles." That optional trip was one I certainly would not repeat.

9
Ministering With Career Missionaries

Japan 1989

SAPPORA, JAPAN, THE SITE OF THE 1972 WINTER Olympics, was also the site of my 1989 mission endeavor. Only ten Americans were fortunate to get to go. Many Japanese Baptist churches backed out of the crusade at the last minute. Door-to-door witnessing is not done in Japan. So each day consisted of planned home meetings where church members invited their unsaved friends into their homes to hear us share our testimonies. Japan was a great example of planting the seed. We did not witness many outward decisions. But the thrill of my heart has been to know that another American partnership with Japan several years later resulted in over 150 decisions. God promised his word will not return void.

Many of us on the crusade felt one of our purposes there was to encourage our own Southern Baptist missionaries. At that point in time they were very discouraged. The cost of living in Japan was escalating rapidly. The cost for a child of our missionaries to attend the International Public School in Tokyo was approximately ten thousand dollars a year which was paid for by our Foreign Mission Board. So, the board was practically demanding that the missionaries home school their children. Some of them shared with me they did not feel personally qualified for the assignment and that it greatly diminished the time they could spend on missionary endeavors. There were also rumors then of pulling missionaries out of Japan and sending them to Brazil or India where there were more visible signs of results. With tears in their eyes, some shared with me their love for the Japanese people and how God had called them to Japan. They were not discouraged because decisions were few and far between. To show their appreciation for us, they had a picnic for the Americans at a beautiful lake near Sappora. They served us watermelon (which they cooled down in a net in the lake). Each watermelon was the size of a huge cantaloupe and cost eighty-five American dollars. We could not even enjoy eating them because we felt as if we were eating gold! I saw cherries in a store for sixty-five dollars. They had small American flags on the wrappers indicating they had been imported.

We did enjoy the fellowship with our missionaries. It was one of the few crusades where we have worked together. We were welcomed to Bucharest, Romania, by two Southern Baptist missionaries. I sadly told my team, "You mark my word. We'll never see them again." And we did not. We needed them as interpreters and to share customs and knowledge of the people. I am so pleased to announce that volunteers and the missionaries in other countries are now encouraged to work together. With the coming of Jerry Rankin to the presidency of the Southern Baptist Foreign Mission Board, the attitude has changed remarkably. The board has formally recognized International Crusades. They are working in harmony with each other. Many of the missionaries welcome a boost to their ministry.

Speaking of boosts, I got a boost to my exercise regime on this trip. My sister Kay accompanied me on this crusade. We took a ten-day side trip to various sites in Japan after the crusade. We were excited about visiting one of our Southern Baptist churches in Kyoto the Sunday we were there. I had called a missionary that Saturday to get directions. These two adventurous sisters set out on the subway on their own early Sunday morning. We got off at our designated location, expecting the church to be about one block away. We walked and walked and walked and walked some more. We were dressed in our "Sunday best—heels and all." Nobody spoke any English, so our attempts to ask directions were futile. Kay learned a lot about her sister that day. I did not give up easily even when dripping with perspiration! We walked until 11:30. Kay almost mutinied on me. I only gave up because we had missed most of the service. I felt better when I was told later that the missionary had given us the wrong stop on the subway.

10

Learning Flexibility in Volunteer Missions

Germany 1989

A S AN OUTGROWTH OF THE LAY RENEWAL WEEKEND that our church experienced in 1989, everyone was invited to the "Cedars of Lebanon" Retreat at Mt. Lebanon, our Baptist encampment near Dallas, over the Labor Day weekend, 1989. Don Gibson shared future plans for lay renewal weekends. Lay teams were going to go into churches for a weekend and share how God was working in their lives.

The Baptist General Convention of Texas was branching out and taking the lay renewal emphasis to Germany to the English-speaking Baptist churches there. That was truly "up my alley." Jim and I had been members of one of those churches for three years while stationed in Germany. I have a special spot in my heart for that ministry because it meant so much to my life while overseas. I remarked to a friend that I would have chosen that trip over Japan had I known earlier. A lay renewal weekend could have so much potential there. The churches labor under many difficulties not experienced by stateside churches. For example, many lose much of their membership every three years due to families rotating back to the United States. Back in the 1960s, they had no way to advertise or get the word out that they even existed. They were not allowed access to the *Stars and Stripes*, the newspaper for American military personnel or to the Armed Forces Network.

Before the retreat closed, I was told that Don Gibson wanted to see me. When I tracked him down, he appeared very excited, but dead serious. He wanted me for the lay renewal team in Germany. He had been alerted that we were retired military people. He was emphatic that I could relate to those churches like no one else. I shared that I would love to go but that my mission budget had been spent in Japan that year. Don pleaded with me to make him a promise—to pray about it for one week. I agreed. Before the week was over, a call came from Don's secretary. Fifty percent of my trip had been donated. Could I come up with the other 50 percent? I answered affirmatively.

We had our first lay renewal weekend in Trinity Baptist Church, Stuttgart, Germany. Mel and Nancy Skinner served there. Mel shared with me how God had called them to be missionaries in Russia. How strange! They asked for Germany because that was the closest they could get to Russia. By the way, they were one of the first couples appointed to Russia when Southern Baptists were admitted. In 1989, who would have thought that was even a remote possibility? Speaking of possibilities, who would have thought I would be in Germany when the Berlin wall came down? I had visited Berlin and East Berlin in 1964. Then, on November 9, 1989, I was in Germany and experienced the excitement—icing on the cake—for this mission trip, a miracle indeed!

The second week we moved to the International Baptist Church. The majority of Americans went on a sightseeing excursion during the week. Because I had already visited all the places they were going, I elected to stay in Stuttgart and offered to go visiting for the church or do whatever they needed me to do. But the Lord has a sense of humor. I guess he felt I needed to be humbled. I was put on a painting detail. Me—on a painting crew. You must be kidding! I had never painted in my life. (I knew the Lord was getting me ready for retirement. When Jim and I retire, we plan to travel in our travel trailer with Campers on Mission, a Christian organization of campers serving under the Southern Baptist Home Mission Board. They do a lot of painting at encampments, and other such jobs. The wives participate in the projects.)

So now, I am an experienced painter. I did not develop a love for it, but I enjoyed the fellowship of the military wives.

The International Baptist Church will be one of the few remaining churches in the area as the American military presence dwindles in Germany. They have a large American contingency. Services are translated into German. They also have many Americans who are civilians, such as IBM employees. My greatest thrill was seeing the growth of the work since we had left in 1963. At that time, there were forty churches. This time, there were about sixty-five. (In the 1960s, the work was not recognized by the Foreign Mission Board. We had a difficult time securing pastors. Not many could pay their own way over, ship their own household goods, and live in Germany on the measly salary paid by small struggling churches. Hamburger meat sold for a dollar a pound in 1963. The pastors could not shop at American military commissaries. Not many of them were foreign missionaries. The Foreign Mission Board is now supporting that work.)

Don Gibson was right. I had instant camaraderie with the military community. The Lord gave me a different type of testimony to meet the needs of these lonely military wives—recalling experiences I had had over twenty years earlier when he had been very near and dear to me in times of difficulty that all military wives and mothers have when living overseas. In a later chapter, the statement, "God's rescue is never early, but never late," will appear, but it could also refer to the following story.

When my husband was stationed in Germany in the military, I became the church pianist when our church split. There was no one who could play. Six weeks before I was planning to leave to rotate back to the States, there was still no one available. I began to feel guilty because I was leaving six weeks before Jim to be home for my sister's high school graduation. The church had been praying; I had been praying. Would you believe, my last Sunday there, someone joined our church who could play the piano. God's word tells us to be anxious for nothing. Many of the members of those tiny struggling churches could identify with my story.

I always loved playing the piano. But I never had any talent for it. My parents knew that, but I insisted on taking lessons. Because

I never had to be prompted to practice, Mother and Dad continued to budget that expensive item, believing they were really throwing away their money. When I wrote them from Germany that I was the church pianist, a whole revelation was revealed to my mother. She said after all those years she now knew why they poured all that money into supporting a whim of mine. God knew back then I would be needed in that small struggling church to play the piano, and he was preparing me for it. Never again would Mother lament over that expenditure that even included organ lessons in high school and college. I have used this illustration sometimes to show that mission endeavors can use those with very minute talents in leadership positions and thereby contribute to Christians' future usefulness to God's kingdom. I am sure my experience helped me be a better pianist in Brazil when I was asked to play for the revival services there. Again, flexibility is the key word on any mission trip.

I was also asked about the church split I had witnessed before. After our pastor had to return to the States, we were using a military lay preacher who volunteered. After several months, he began pushing for his ordination. One of our godly deacons became very burdened. He realized we were not ordaining this man just to be a pastor in Germany; we were putting our stamp of approval on him to return to the United States and become a Baptist pastor. It just so happened the deacon had known this man before his wife joined him in Germany, and he had been unfaithful. So he went to the man and asked him to drop the ordination request, or he would be forced to share his past with the church. Several weeks later, the man left and took most of the congregation with him. Our first Sunday we had three couples, but God is faithful. Before we rotated to the States eighteen months later, the church had one hundred members. Many who left in the split returned.

As a young married couple, we saw how God rewards individuals and churches who are faithful to him and stand up for their convictions. As Don Gibson had so appropriately said, "Your prior experiences in Germany will offer encouragement and hope to those who need renewal on the lay renewal weekend."

11

Serving Without the Comforts of Home

Romania 1991

THIS CRUSADE HAD SPECIAL MEANING FOR ME because Juanita, Jim's aunt, was privileged to accompany me. This was her first trip outside the United States. She could not have selected a better trip to see the contrast between democracy and communism. Our coordinator said he had only been to one country more backward and deprived than Romania; that was Bolivia in South America. The night we spent in Suceava educated us about the water of the country. It came out of the faucet looking and feeling rusty.

The next day, we learned to appreciate the private bath and shower in our room. We boarded a bus to travel to our churches. There were to be four stops. Each stop led us to a more deserted, poverty-stricken area. We knew we were to get off at the last stop. The situation looked really bleak. The third team came back to the bus and asked us to really pray for them. They had already been told the electricity and water were routinely cut off at 8:00 P.M. each night. They would not be back to the hotel until 9:00 or 10:00 each night. When we got to our hotel, the first question asked was, "Do we have water?" The clerk said yes. We were elated. We proceeded to our rooms. All of us were in close proximity. It seemed we all walked to the door at the same time and peered out. We had water all right, but no bath. There was a community toilet at the end of the hall, but no tub or shower. There was only a wash basin the size of a saucepan in each room. Needless to say, we did not need much water that week (just lots of cologne)!

All of our rooms were in one area. Juanita and I were the only ladies rooming together. All others were couples or gentlemen. We were assured of instant attention should we need it. One night we had the opportunity to test their sincerity. We got locked in our room. Only Juanita and Jeannine could do that. We tried for the longest time to escape. The more we tried, the more tickled we became. Why not? It was better to laugh than to cry or panic. (We remembered Proverbs 17:22: "A merry heart doeth good like a medicine.") Finally, we had to admit defeat. So we began calling our neighbors on each side. Silence was not golden that night. We resorted to banging on the walls. After much noise and frustration, a Romanian came to our rescue. Needless to say, we did not let our fellow Americans live that one down. But we did not care to give them a chance to redeem themselves with the antiquated locks and keys we were using.

In case of fire, we did have a window (second floor) at our disposal, but remember that the "pit stop" was down the hall. Remember the critters in Los Angeles? We could hear slightly larger ones at this hotel—rats. That was when I thanked the Lord for the smaller ones that welcomed me to Los Angeles. We never saw our visitors, so we convinced each other they must just be in the walls. We were elated when we would come into our room knowing there had been no maid service that day. They would merely sweep our rug which would just stir up the dust all the more.

I had a wonderful respite from our grungy quarters. I served with a wonderful church. God blessed our efforts each day. Visiting in hospitals, homes, and government offices, we filled our time wisely. Our pastor was prepared for the revival and utilized us to our maximum. I even played the organ, which I had not done since college. (My parents' money spent on organ lessons paid off finally.)

One memory stands out about this church: They worshiped with all windows closed. It was very hot with no air-conditioning.

They would not so much as crack a window. They had worshiped for so long in fear for their lives under communism. We tried to tell them if they would open the windows people would hear us singing and come in to see what we were doing. But that fear could not be overcome.

The most meaningful moment of this crusade was the closing rally in Suceava. An American and a Romanian spoke. When the Romanian stood to speak, we found out why there was a big hole in the middle of the Romanian flag. His closing statement, as he placed his Bible through the hole in the center of the flag was this: "You have come to Romania to show us we must fill the gap with God's Word. To you, we make that promise. The gap that came with the fall of communism will be met with the knowledge of Jesus Christ."

We boarded our bus the next morning for the airport to start our lengthy trip home when we received the startling news that Gorbachev had been dethroned and godless communism had met its defeat in Russia. Would the Lord bring some of us back to eastern Europe soon to repeat his victories he so generously poured out in Romania? As we prayed and thanked God that he is in control, we knew Russia would be the next crusade for many of us. Stay tuned for further developments!

12
Visiting Those in Prison

Russia 1992

I N 1991, THE GOD WHO CRUSHED THE WALLS OF JERICHO sent a chariot of fire thundering through the doors of the Soviet Union. And souls held captive for more than seventy years were finally set free. But God's chariot didn't stop there. It began an incredible journey. A journey that would change the body of Christ forever. A journey that would gather ordinary Christians for an extraordinary calling . . . to help the people of the former Soviet Union rebuild their society on the truth of God's Word."[1]

Standing in Red Square singing "How Great Thou Art"—what a phenomenal event! Only the Lord could bring such an occurrence to pass. I am so grateful to God for such an awesome experience.

As I made plans to go to Russia with 138 Americans, Cecil Peasley, the South African evangelist, came to Dallas. He inquired where my next mission trip would take me. When I answered, "Russia," he shared he would be with International Crusades on that same trip. Later, I told Jim how nice it would be if we could be on the same team. He suggested I call International Crusades and ask to be on his team. I refused. As I mentioned in earlier chapters, I pray for the coordinators who place each team together. I really leave it in the Lord's hands. When the letter from International

Crusades arrived, I discovered I was on Cecil's team. I assumed that Cecil had called and requested I serve with him. When we met in Russia, I asked him if this had been the case. He was assuming that I had called. I said, "No, the Lord did it." Icing on the cake, again!

Landing in Moscow was such a foreboding experience. It was more bleak than India. Everything was so antiquated. There were practically no lights in the airport. The luggage carousel squeaked and was in such ill repair that we wondered if our luggage would ever come through. We rode a train all night to Nizhni Novgorod. I was blessed with dry sheets on the bed; some had wet sheets. Sanitary conditions brought back memories of India. Needless to say, it was a long night. We did have one bright spot. There were two Soviet soldiers on the train. A retired United States colonel and I had the opportunity to witness to them. With our military background, we again had instant communication with them. I loved the colonel's testimony that he shared later with us. He said he had spent twenty years of his life learning ways to destroy Russia— land and people. He was now there to share God's love with the Russians and tell them how they could be saved.

After an all-night ride, we boarded a bus for an all-day bus ride. The bus was a 1940s vintage with no maintenance since then. My previous prayers had to suffice because the Lord had other plans for me during the bus ride. Our coordinator in orientation always said we needed to be "prayed up" before departing on a crusade.

We were told ahead of time that our interpreters would probably not be Christians. Most of them were English students from Moscow University. It is really important that your interpreter be a Christian because that person is so crucial to your ministry. We made that a matter of prayer before the crusade. Sure enough, our interpreters were not. So during that day-long bus ride, I had the opportunity to share Christ with those two young ladies; both accepted him as we chugged along to the edge of civilization.

Our destination was Nizhni Lomov, eleven hundred miles from Moscow. When we got off the bus, we were in the middle of nowhere on a dirt road with deep chuckholes. I found out that wheels on luggage do not cooperate on gravel roads. We walked until we thought we could not take another step. We finally arrived at our hotel. It was a government hotel where men stayed during the week while they worked in a nearby factory. When they assigned our rooms, I was given a room on one floor while our two interpreters Cecil and Leighton were on another. While I had no qualms in Romania of traipsing down the hall to the toilet amidst some undesirable characters, my antennas immediately went up. For some reason, I felt very uneasy. I conferred with Cecil Peasley concerning my anxiety. He agreed we should all be together on one floor. To do this, we moved furniture and rearranged rooms, thoroughly confusing the hotel staff. I am sure they thought, "Those crazy Americans." The very next night someone tried to enter our interpreter's room. I was thankful for the Lord's physical protection.

We soon learned that this was one crusade where organization and planning had been nonexistent. Some Russian people have been programmed by others for so long they do not comprehend organization of any kind. The preliminary trip revealed this problem, and we were prepared to be flexible. Our team fared better than others since all of us were experienced crusaders. So we "took the ball and ran with it." We led our pastor to make appointments for us in schools, hospitals, and nursing homes. In Romania, our pastor always said, "No problem." Any idea we had, he let us implement it. In Russia, we said everything became a problem. Our interpreters and the pastor would discuss any situation at great lengths. Sometimes, we would be sorry that we ever brought something up. The pastor was a joy to work with, but everything was so difficult to implement. He pastored four churches because there are not enough pastors. Four hundred pastors are needed.

We assumed our pastor was securing taxis for us. About the middle of the week, I asked how he knew they were taxis since nothing on the vehicle indicated it. I wish I had not asked. They were not taxis. He was just thumbing rides for us. In other words, we were hitchhiking everywhere we went. One night, our driver was drunk. But everything is relative. Remember, I've been to Rio de Janeiro, Mexico City, and India. At least in Russia, there are not as many vehicles to collide with as in other countries.

I always call Jim at the halfway mark during each mission trip. This was not a problem until these eastern European trips. During our Romanian orientation meeting, we were told to forget about calling home and to alert our families in advance. Walking around our hotel in Rodauti, Romania, on our first night there, we met two Americans from Dallas. Small world, huh? They were there for the summer representing the Christ for the Nations Institute in Dallas. They spotted us about a week later, very exuberant, and could not wait to tell us they had called family in Dallas. They instructed us to go to the post office. You could not use any credit cards or call collect. You told the clerk how long you wanted to talk. I said five minutes instead of our usual ten minutes (knocking off five minutes for fear of cost). She put the call through, and in five minutes Jim was on the line. The call cost three dollars. I was absolutely shocked. My previous calls usually averaged about twenty dollars for ten minutes. If I had known it would only be three dollars, I would have chatted for twenty minutes.

Our visit to the mayor's office proved exciting for me. In Nizhni Lomov, the only phone in the city was in his office. After our visit, he asked if there was anything he could do for any of us. Cecil Peasley knew my habit of calling home as our spokesman, he casually remarked (really joking) that I would like to call my husband. This was no sooner said than done—some more icing on the cake!

We had the unusual opportunity to go into a prison. Speaking and witnessing in a prison is much like witnessing on a plane. You have a captive audience. The prisoners were visibly moved that we would be willing to endure a long bus ride to such a desolate location to share the love of God with them. (When we were pulling our luggage over those chuckholes, we just thought that was at the end of civilization.) Prisons were meant to be well isolated from communities, but we did have the bus. Another day, my interpreter asked me if I would be willing to go see a friend so she could witness to her. Did you read my words? She would witness. Indeed, she had caught the vision! We walked and we walked some more. (I now wear a pedometer on my trips.) We walked almost two hours. We walked until my stomach muscles were sore. That was certainly a new experience for me. I was glad she was doing the witnessing because I did not have much breath or energy left. But God never gives us more than we can bear. We claim that promise mostly when we have tragedy or heartbreak in our lives, but you learn that applies to physical strength also. We had four people on this crusade over eighty years of age. My interpreter had her first convert that day. Somehow, the walk back did not seem as long.

When we linked up with fellow Americans in Penza on our way back to Moscow, our first reaction was, "Do I look that bad?" We could use no makeup or jewelry on this crusade. Our heads had to be covered inside the church. Russian Christians do not wear makeup. It is the "mark of the world" to them. I was glad to get a few extra minutes of sleep each day (not having to put on "my face"). It was a hang-up to a few Americans. Some refused to remove their makeup. It created quite a stir, ruining the reputation of all of us. Perhaps they forgot Paul's admonition to become all things to all men in order to save some. My interpreters wore earrings when I met them. Almost immediately after their conversion, I observed the earrings were gone.

When we returned to Moscow, we were taken to McDonald's, the largest one in the world. We wondered what organization would be there. They have about twenty-five registers, and everything moved swiftly. The employees are trained by Americans. Unlike other places, it is safe there to have ice in your cokes. Needless to say, most of us ordered two to three drinks. After having nothing but cucumbers and potatoes for two weeks, a Big Mac hit the spot. The man sitting next to me divulged that he never went to McDonald's in the States, but that that was the best hamburger he had had in many a moon. I had an identical testimony. I keep saying God puts teams and locations together.

I like cucumbers. Existing on cucumbers and potatoes was not a problem for me (even though I would rather not have had them for breakfast.) Those were the two items grown in the area of Nizhni Lomov. Other teams subsisted on carrots and potatoes.

Cabbage and potatoes were on the menu for some teams. Several told me they would have been in a heap of trouble had cucumbers been their fare since cucumbers disagree with them. The Lord knew I could lose a few pounds and enjoy cucumbers, so I was chosen to go to Nizhni Lomov.

The postscript to this story follows: When I returned, we were dining with friends who wanted to keep me humble. While waiting for our food to come, they presented me gifts—a cucumber and a potato. There were 11,369 decisions recorded as a result of 138 people and 30 churches responding to the Great Commission.

NOTE

1. *The Chariot* (quarterly newsletter of the CoMission Prayer Committee, Wheaton, Ill.), vol. 5, no. 3, 1995.

13
Ministering Through the Association of Christian Schools International
Russia 1993

R EMEMBER WHEN I SAID THAT I NEVER CARE TO GO back to a place a second time? Read on. My Lord certainly does not agree with my rationale. In November each year, I attend the Association of Christian Schools International (ACSI) Convention. One seminar dealt with a mission endeavor to Russia using Christian schoolteachers. I attended this seminar out of curiosity just to see what was going on in Russia that could use American teachers. During the first thirty minutes of the presentation, I knew I was on my way back to Russia. The testimonies melted my dogmatic spirit.

Campus Crusade for Christ had been asked by the Russian Department of Education to hold convocations for the Russian schoolteachers to teach Bible curriculum ("Christian Ethics and Morality") to the teachers. They, in turn, would teach it to their students. ACSI supplied the teachers. I was shocked to hear the cost of the trip. It was twice what I had paid in July to go. So after the presentation, I asked the leader privately why it was so costly. She answered, "We eat American style." That really rubbed me the wrong way. I retorted, "Well, we ate Russian style." I was really perturbed because I feel that is how Americans earn the term "ugly American." Many feel they are too good to eat as the nationals.

Afterward, I thought, "Boy, I blew that. With my attitude, I won't be going." They probably did not want me, but the Lord did. He has a way of humbling us. I had to repent. I learned what was meant by eating American style. We ate "controlled food." That meant a representative from Campus Crusade and a Russian went into every place we ate. They told the manager what we would eat, where it would be bought, and how it would be cooked. Therefore, everything was safe. For example, we could even eat salad because the lettuce had been washed in purified water. Only one person out of sixty-five got sick on the trip. Because of our heavy teaching responsibilities, no one could afford to be sick. We also paid for the Russian teachers' meals. Otherwise, they would not be able to come to the convocations. We presented many books, such as Josh McDowell's *Evidence Demands a Verdict*, to the teachers.

I was assigned to the convocation October 13–November 1 at Murmansk and Tver. I love to locate Murmansk on a globe. Just go to the top of the globe. It is four hundred miles north of the Arctic Circle. The Lord keeps proving to me that I was wrong when I thought I was at the farthest point of civilization: India, Nizhni Lomov, and now Murmansk. It is on the Barents Sea. With the wind coming off the sea, the chill factor was about minus thirty degrees. We wore layers upon layers of clothing. I would usually wear a wool pants suit with a wool shell, then add a bulky sweater and my heavy winter coat. I had fur-lined boots and a fur hat. I looked like a mummy. I had taken a ski mask, but was told it did not look professional. We were instructed to look professional. We wore dresses to the convocations and had to shed our boots for dress pumps. The teaching profession evokes more respect in Russia than in the United States. That is why it was important to have teachers on the convocations. Others could go; we had a lawyer on our trip. But teachers have more credibility with the Russian educators.

Each convocation averaged around three hundred teachers. The day began with everyone together in a large cultural hall (similar to our convention center). There was a preliminary session. A topic such as "A Christian Worldview" would be explored. The "Walk Through the Bible" organization presented a

The Kirov Culture and Technology Palace

monologue familiarizing the audience with the Bible. On the third day, a film would be shown documenting the life of Christ. It was so dynamic that even viewing it in Russian was a blessing to my life. As of 1994, 528 million people had seen the film with 34 million indicating a decision to receive Christ. It has been made available in 282 languages and shown in 201 countries.

Then we shared lunch together. Lunch was two miles away in a Russian school. We were delighted to visit the different schools, but less than enthusiastic about the walk. We had to walk up an extremely steep hill which was solid ice. After the first day, many decided to bring a snack and stay at the Cultural Hall. That was nixed by our coordinator. Lunchtime was to be a get-acquainted period with the Russian teachers. We inquired if there was a possibility of the tour bus transporting us to the school. It was such a dangerous two miles. One American fell and suffered a mild concussion the first day. However, the coordinator reminded us there was not room for the Russian teachers on the bus and that it would not look good for the Americans to ride to lunch and the Russians to walk. So, we proved we were not wimpy and became rather proficient at "sliding" to lunch each day.

The afternoons were spent in workshops in the three tracks—administrative, elementary, and secondary. I was assigned to the administrative. I had no experience in administration, but sometimes I believe the Lord chooses to stretch us. And I had learned from my first mission trip to be flexible. The director of each track would give an overview of the lesson. Then we would divide into small groups of eight to ten and discuss the topic. At the end of the afternoon, we would come back together for a sharing time and wrap-up by the director.

Our evenings were spent in relaxation, usually with our interpreters. Schools in the area presented musical programs such as choirs and ballets. One night I was asked to be on a panel with the topic of "Parent-Teacher Organizations in the United States." I was asked to discuss the role of room mothers, fund-raising, field trips, and related topics. One evening, our interpreter took us to her home for dinner. I climbed 252 steps to her home. I call that working for my dinner. By the way, I only walked down 250, slipping on two of them and spraining my wrist. Can you imagine wearing an ace bandage in addition to your pants suit jacket, sweater, and coat? More fun! I told you we looked like mummies. I wanted to look more authentic. An ace bandage was the extra touch I needed.

I cannot say enough about our interpreters. They were the best. Most were university professors. One who interpreted for the preliminary morning sessions is the voice for CNN. Until the Jesus film was shown the third day, we were not allowed to discuss Christianity. We were strictly professional teachers discussing ethics and morality. We were to gain respect professionally. Then, after the Jesus film, we shared our personal testimony and witnessed to each one in our small groups. One of the group's homework assignments was to draw a road map depicting their spiritual journey. The next day they all came back with a literal road map of Murmansk. Now they know how their students feel when they mess up on a homework assignment. Another misinterpretation occurred when the word "headset" became "handcuffs." I told them to put on their headsets; they thought I said put on your handcuffs.

The next week we moved to a warmer climate—in Tver—for the next convocation. Tver is 150 miles northwest of Moscow. We were thankful for a tour bus for the four-hour trip to Tver from Moscow, having flown on Aeroflot from Murmansk. You have not experienced adventure until you have flown Aeroflot. When we boarded the plane, we were told to sit up front because all of our luggage was in the back. It had to all balance out. That was encouraging and gave us real confidence. We were informed the pilots were some of the best trained in the world, most being former Soviet Air Force pilots. But maintenance was not high on their priority list. (In the past year an Aeroflot flight crashed. The pilot was allowing his teenage son to fly the plane. So experience is obviously not a priority either.)

One of our group discovered an unattached seat belt, and he held it up for the flight attendant to see. She came by, stuffed it back down in the seat, and told him to fasten it. Real comfort, huh? (I apologize for any derogatory statements about Aeroflot. I did not know I had it so good. Stay tuned for the chapter on China.)

Tver is a very old city—older than Moscow. It has many castles and churches and is on the Volga River. It is a very anti-American city. Several of the Americans were spit on while walking in town. It is still a communist stronghold. We were instructed to leave the hotel only in groups of six or more. Campus Crusade put a guard in our hotel lobby. Conditions later warranted security on each floor. Finally, the ladies were told not to leave their rooms without an escort. Our floor had a total of four men and ten ladies.

Campus Crusade had a busy time keeping up with all of us, supplying us with water and other needs. But the organization kept us supplied with purified water. That was a real blessing. The hotels in Brazil, Mexico, and India had all provided bottled water, but during the time we were in Romania and Russia, there was no bottled water. They were not geared for tourism. The large cities now have it. We took our own purifiers to Romania and Russia. (See Appendix II for more information on purifiers.) Campus Crusade had five-gallon commercial purifiers attached to their showers at night and then distributed our water to us each morning. So the ladies appreciated our "water boys." We appreciated the alertness of Campus Crusade to the difficult situation and the decisions they made to protect us. Most of all, we thanked the Lord for physical protection.

We enjoyed the friendship we made with the CoMission teams. We merely introduced the curriculum in the four-day convocations. Then, a CoMission team followed us and stayed in the area one year to implement the curriculum in each school. They showed the Jesus film to parent meetings and similar organizations. They initiated Bible study groups in neighborhoods and civic centers. They followed up on decisions made for Christ at the convocations and later. They instructed the teachers on how to disciple new converts.

The teams became a link with the Russian Orthodox Church. This was very important. The Russian Orthodox Church has been a real hindrance to the Christian cause in Russia. In fact, when I was in Nizhni Lomov, they attempted to sabotage our meetings. During all the years of communism, the nation was told lies, such as the claim that Baptists were killing the babies. Many false rumors were circulated about Christians and Baptists in particular. There is so much animosity that many Baptists told me they believe the Russian Orthodox Church will be their next force of persecution. In Nizhni Lomov they told residents all the Americans were crazy and not to come hear us. We attempted to meet them and discuss the situation, but their priests would not meet with us. Because Campus Crusade is interdenominational, they have been able to earn their confidence. We even had a Russian Orthodox priest speak at our plenary sessions each day. The CoMission teams attempted to work closely with them.

It is not always possible to secure a CoMission team for each city that has a convocation. There just are not enough volunteers. Many teachers cannot give up a year of teaching, earn their support for one year, and take their spouse and children to Russia for the year. Children have to be home schooled at the beginning. Now there are some Christian schools being established for the children of missionaries and CoMission volunteers. I am so excited to know Tver has a CoMission team.

Winter Palace (now the State Hermitage) in St. Petersburg

One of our last projects before we departed Russia was to clean out our suitcases and leave all peanut butter, snacks, toilet paper, and other such goodies for the CoMission teams. There is no way for them to take enough of these precious commodities with them to last a year. I am wondering how long sixty-five jars of peanut butter and sixty-five rolls of toilet paper lasts them! Those of us who could left clothing for the parents of the Russian students. This gave the Russian teachers an entrée into the homes of their students to share Christ with the parents. Some remnants of my wardrobe are in Nizhni Lomov also. In Romania there was a great need for clothes also, but I did not go prepared to leave mine. Now I select my wardrobe with that in mind. (It is an easy way to keep closets cleaned out and an excuse to buy new clothes.)

As of April 1, 1996, 2,900 Americans had participated in 109 convocations with 34,023 public educators trained. Fifty percent of them have accepted Christ. Ninety percent were actually teaching the curriculum. Praise the Lord! With the very real danger of the government canceling convocations (which has already begun happening), the CoMission teams are training the Russian administrators to conduct the convocations. Is that not the purpose of all missionaries—to work ourselves out of a job as the nationals assume the responsibility of winning their own to Christ?

I want to close this chapter by printing three stories. The first comes from a recent issue of *The Comobilizer* (a publication of Campus Crusade for Christ's Convocation and CoMission offices, Orlando, Florida):

A Day in the Life

In the 1930s, Stalin ordered a purge of all Bibles and all believers. In Stavropol, Russia, this order was carried out with a vengeance. Thousands of Bibles were confiscated and multitudes of believers were sent to the "gulags"—prison camps where most died for being "enemies of the state."

Last year, CoMission sent a team to Stavropol. The city's history wasn't known at that time. But, when our team was having difficulty getting Bibles shipped from Moscow, someone mentioned the existence of a warehouse outside of town where these confiscated Bibles had been stored since Stalin's day.

After much prayer by the team, one member finally got up the courage to go to the warehouse and ask the officials if the Bibles were still there. Sure enough, they were. Then the CoMissioners asked if the Bibles could be removed and distributed again to the people of Stavropol. The answer was "Yes."

The next day the CoMission team returned with a truck and several Russian helpers to help load the Bibles. One helper was a young man—a skeptical, agnostic, hostile collegian who had come only for the day's wages. As they were loading Bibles, one team member noticed that the young man had disappeared. Eventually they found him in a corner of the warehouse, weeping.

He had slipped away, hoping to quietly take a Bible for himself. What he found shook him to the core.

The inside page of the Bible he picked up had the handwritten signature of his own grandmother. It had been her personal Bible. Out of the thousands of Bibles left in that warehouse, he stole one belonging to his grandmother, a woman persecuted all her life for her faith.

No wonder he was weeping—God was real. His grandmother had no doubt prayed for him and her city. His discovery of this Bible is only a glimpse into the spirit realm—and this young man is in the process of being transformed by the very Bible that his grandmother found so dear.

Here's the story of one U.S. CoMission team and an experience they had with one Russian teacher taken from a recent issue of CoMission's newsletter, *The Chariot*:

What is happening in Russia is truly unbelievable apart from God's presence and the work of His Spirit. We simply had an opportunity to join Him there. The doors He has opened for the teams are incredible. Our people have taught Bible on a military installation (the first Americans ever allowed on this base). They teach English at a scientific institute to some of the intellectual elite in all of Russia. They teach Bible to children in the community center (which used to be a Communist Pioneer Palace). They have Bible studies with different groups in several flats (simultaneously) almost every day. All this in addition to the work in the schools!

There is also a regular prison ministry at a prison two hours north by train. The commandant of the prison offered to *give* the team a house if they would move there and minister full time! The team turns down more offers than they accept and has a long waiting list of schools wanting them to come. The fields are truly "white unto harvest and the laborers are few."

The last story (also found in a recent issue of *The Chariot*), told by Paul Eshleman, director for the *JESUS* Film Project, begins by asking the question, "Would You Commute Seven Hours *One Way*?"

"When Kurt and Elke and their team arrived in the Ukraine, they were treated almost as heroes. They were the first Westerners ever to set foot on the campuses where they worked. Elke appeared regularly on the local television news and interview shows to explain what they were doing in the city and how people could live by the moral and ethical teachings of Jesus taken from the Bible.

"But it was not an easy assignment; they had left a lot of conveniences behind. They were in a city with no supermarkets, no malls, no Laundromats and no McDonald's. And they lived in a tiny apartment where they rejoiced when the elevator worked and the water ran hot.

"During the day, they held classes for teachers in various schools on teaching the *Christian Ethics and Morality* curriculum. One wonderful result of these classes is that many teachers came to faith in Christ. So Kurt and Elke also held Bible studies for converted teachers to help them grow in their own personal faith. In the evenings, they showed the *JESUS* Film to parents, and began follow-up Bible studies in the parents' homes.

"In one of the schools where Elke worked, a new teacher (we'll call her Olga) showed up about four weeks into the class. Elke introduced herself and learned that Olga had traveled *seven hours* to be there because she had heard about Elke's class.

"Elke handed her a copy of every resource she had—the *Christian Ethics and Morality* curriculum, Josh McDowell's book on the resurrection, and finally a Bible. Olga started to weep. She said it was the first time she had ever held a Bible in her hands. She didn't know what to say.

"Week after week, once a week, Olga traveled the seven hours in the morning, stayed for Elke's hour-and-a-half class, and then traveled the seven hours back to her home. When Elke asked her what she was doing with the information she was gaining, Olga said that each Monday she taught the other teachers in her school what she had learned from Elke!

"Eventually, Elke and Kurt actually got to visit Olga's school and showed Bill Bright's video, *Man Without Equal*. The response was wonderful, and Olga is continuing to teach the Bible to those who have responded.

"Elke commended, 'I have never seen people so hungry to know God.'"

An update on CoMission: 19 teams, 129 CoMissioners, and 25 children departed the United States in January 1996. That brings the total to 250 who have stayed for the one year CoMission commitment.

More icing on the cake. My Sunday School teacher, Gene Merrell, was in Russia the same time I was. Upon settling in for the long transatlantic flight home, I heard my name called. I thought, "Who could that be? I don't know any team member traveling to Dallas." To my utter amazement, it was Gene. We were both ecstatic. We could not wait to begin sharing how God had blessed the two very distinct ministries. (He had lectured at a Russian University.) That was the shortest transatlantic flight I have ever experienced. We talked nonstop most of the trip. It was such a blessing!

14

Teaching Conversational English

Poland 1994

F ARLA SIMPKINS, ONE OF MY WONDERFUL FRIENDS from Campers on Missions (our Christian camping organization affiliated with the Southern Baptist Home Mission Board) sent me a brochure. Michael Gott had led a revival in their church in Greenville, Texas, and made a plea for people to go to Poland with him to teach conversational English in the Baptist churches. She thought I might be interested. It has been fascinating for me to see how God has called me in different ways for each trip. While I was at an orientation meeting at Mt. Lebanon, I had the pleasure of meeting Michael's wife Jan. Each summer she leads a Vacation Bible School at Interlaken, Switzerland (the "Ridgecrest" of the European Baptist Convention). Again, I began reliving my memories of Interlaken when I was a member of the English-speaking church in Germany. This was another opportunity for me to invest my life in the European ministry.

I believe so strongly that the Lord leads each coordinator to assign us exactly where the Lord needs us. A few days before we departed, Jan called to ask me if I would be willing to go to a different city in Poland than originally planned. I immediately agreed. A few moments later, Juanita Patterson, who was scheduled to be my room-mate, called from California to say she did not react as positively to

Parliament Building in Budapest

Jan as I had. She was not going to go. She wanted to work with a couple we had met at orientation. I was very perplexed. Praying daily, I never felt peace. I left Dallas, leaving it in God's hands.

After a great sightseeing trip in Budapest, Hungary, and an opportunity to worship at the Baptist church in Budapest, we arrived in Interlaken by train from Zurich having flown from Budapest. By divine appointment, we had dinner with Juanita's favorite couple, and they shared how there was a desperate need for two more people to go to Eblag and how we just must be flexible on mission trips. Returning to our room, I shared how I felt God was giving us one more chance to say yes to his will. Again, there was no agreement. Juanita left the room to get some coffee with the terse remark, "I may just return to the States with the Interlaken group." What a dilemma! Should I run my roommate off and follow what seemed to be the Lord's leading or take a good assignment instead of the best? The Lord allows us to make that choice. He wants the best for us, but we sometimes settle for less.

To make a long story short, after a two-hour break, Juanita returned to say Eblag would be our destination. I was thankful for the assurance that we would be partaking of God's best in Poland. Many prayers were answered during those two hours.

We had a great Vacation Bible School (170 children). One of my children was from the Hanau church where we had been members. We had observed much turmoil in the military community. Fourteen churches had closed due to the closing of so many military installations in Europe. I learned that the Ninety-seventh General Hospital in Frankfurt, where my son had been born, had closed. Rhein Main Air Force Base (the Hub), which was the processing headquarters for all military personnel arriving and departing Europe, was closing. Jan met a father bringing his child to Vacation Bible School. The father had been saved as a child attending Vacation Bible School when his parents were stationed in Germany. Trips to Bern, Lucern, Grundelwald, Brientz, and Schilthorn Peak all occurred during our afternoons. After a fun-filled week of Vacation Bible School, we flew to Warsaw and took a bus to Eblag.

The team was from Metropolitan Baptist Church in Houston, Texas. The pastor for the week was none other than Michael Gott—again, icing on the cake. Each day started with a large group time. We learned how to be fools for Christ's sake as we sang crazy songs and performed for our students. This showed them that Christians could have fun and helped them to relax and not be so uptight when they made mistakes trying to speak English.

We divided into beginner, intermediate, and advanced small groups. I was assigned to one of the advanced small groups. The basic class learned the colors, shapes, and some basic language concepts. The advanced had more freedom and fun. They learned how to fill out a job application. They interviewed for jobs. There is an understanding in Poland that to be successful in the future, you must know English. Thus, to make the classes practical, we taught job etiquette, job skills, and other practical applications. We assigned newspaper articles and travel brochures for them to read. We had fun topics for them to write on such as "What was your most embarrassing moment?" and "What was your favorite

Museum of Stutthof—a former concentration camp

vacation?" They also performed skits for us in English.

Because we had all ages, we had to have the school at night. Many were adults who worked during the day. So we decided on the spur of the moment to have a Vacation Bible School each morning. I have never seen Vacation Bible School come together so quickly with so few supplies and no literature.

Think for a moment. We were in Poland, a foreign country, gathering supplies in a language we did not speak. The Lord has a terrific sense of humor. But we triumphed. We met ninety children the next day with Bible stories prepared, memory verses selected, craft ideas galore, and smiling faces. It is exciting to see God work when you make yourself available. Juanita did not realize there was a reason for all the experience she received in Vacation Bible School that summer. Since she had no children, God was preparing her to take care of my granddaughter. She baby-sits full time now.

While the ladies were conducting Vacation Bible School, the men went into prisons to share the gospel. There did not seem to be any idle moments for anyone. On Saturday, we took the students by bus on a field trip to a castle—Malbork—climbing to the top via 275-plus steps. This participant was ready. Remember the 252 steps in Russia? The Lord seems to give me a challenge on each crusade. Who should we meet at the top but Michael Gott? I asked him if he

Monument of Fight and Freedom in ex-concentration camp in Stutthof

had come up to administer the last rites to us? During the field trip, we had a picnic for our students. This gave us more quality time in an informal setting to become better friends with them.

The agenda was much like the one in Russia. We did not discuss Christianity the first week. We gained their confidence in our status as teachers. Then the second week, we held the revival service at the church each evening, with several of us sharing our personal testimonies during the service. One night after the revival, we treated them to a campfire, where we roasted marshmallows and served "s'mores." The graham crackers and marshmallows had traveled all the way from Houston, Texas. American customs and southern hospitality were a big hit with our new Polish friends.

We were introduced to Andre, a doctor. He had traveled to the United States to study. He was won to Christ by a local resident in his city and taken to a Baptist church. He is now a key contact for Michael Gott in coordinating all the work in Poland. We need to be cognizant of our opportunities to witness to foreigners in our own country. The United States is a mission field in more ways than one. So many return to their countries as missionaries to their own people. What a blessing!

Andre shared with us some Baptist history in Poland: "The Baptist movement started in Poland in 1858 when some people near Warsaw came together for Bible study and prayer in a private house. Before the Second World War, there were two groups: the German Baptist Union and the Slavic Baptist Association. Both groups had about 20,000 members. The war destroyed everything. Polish Baptists started with 1,500 members. In spite of continuing immigration, the number of Baptists is growing every year. Currently, there are 56 Baptist churches and over 50 mission stations with 3,217 adult baptized members."

There are now sixty more believers. One hundred took the English class. It was a great success. Many in my church told me it could not be done in two weeks because they usually teach conversational English for six months for each class. Five schools were held that summer with more than one hundred decisions, and those students departed speaking English!

15
Traveling via World Help

China 1995

S OMETIMES I BELIEVE I AM ON EVERY CHRISTIAN organization's mailing list. Out of curiosity, I usually scan the material before filing it in "File 13." I received a brochure from World Help, but that brochure never made it to File 13. I stacked it away and ever so often pondered over it. Finally, I knew I had to get serious with myself and admit I was headed to China. But with World Help? I never heard of the organization. Traveling without Jim, I like to travel with reputable organizations.

According to a brochure, I knew World Help was endorsed by Bill Bright of Campus Crusade for Christ and Jay Strack who was vice-president of the Southern Baptist Convention. I did not think I could get through to Bill Bright, so I phoned Jay Strack. I asked for his opinion of World Help. It was glowing. He ended our lengthy conversation with this remark: "If it will make you feel any better, our organization just sent that organization a three-thousand-dollar check. I travel almost exclusively with them." Having prayed before the call, I knew that was God's assurance that I would travel with yet another wonderful ministry.

World Help was founded in 1991. So far, nine hundred people have gone overseas with them. World Help is closely associated with Liberty University, Lynchburg, Virginia. Vernon Brewer, president of

World Help, was on the staff. They use many Liberty students on the four to five trips they take each year to Russia, China, and Romania. I received a new appreciation for that university. I have never seen such mature Christian young people. Many of them had never been out of the United States. To face situations we faced, they really exhibited their love for Christ. My roommate was a nineteen-year-old student. My husband teased me before I left saying she was not going to enjoy rooming with someone old enough to be her mother. Do you know her initial remark to me? "I have been praying that I could room with an older lady because the Bible says older women shall teach the younger. I know I can learn so much from you." How many college students would have those feelings? Our coordinator was a twenty-eight-year-old graduate of Liberty. To be responsible for twenty Americans going into Mainland China is an awesome task. He was superb!

Jim and I had been to Wichita, Kansas, to visit our son David and his wife Joetta. We made a special point to be back in Dallas for a prayer of commitment on the Sunday before I was to leave. I shared with my church what I would be doing in China such as taking Bibles into Mainland China. When we returned home that night, I had my final instructions from World Help (having been gone four days). To my horror I read, "Please do not tell exactly what you will be doing in China." Wow! I had just told the world. Our church services are broadcast on the radio. Sometimes, the service ends at the invitation. I called someone to see if I had been so fortunate. No, they confirmed everything I said had gone over the airways. I heard remarks such as, "I hope you didn't jeopardize your trip," and "You should call World Help and inform them."

I was really burdened that night and prayed earnestly. I made the decision not to do anything, and this was why: It is very difficult for me to go to the front of the church and ask for prayer. Remember the introduction to this book? I am an introvert; I am shy and do not feel comfortable in front of people. But I know I must do it; I do want people praying for me. Besides, the Lord taught me a lesson long ago. The India Crusade was the first one where I was the only one from my church going. I confess I did not follow the Holy Spirit's prompting to go down during the invitation.

The next day, when Ben Mieth called to tell me my passport did not arrive from Houston, the first thought that came to me was the Holy Spirit's chastisement: "You thought you didn't need prayer; now look at the mess you are in." I had to ask for forgiveness, and I vowed never to make that mistake again. Because it was such an ordeal for me, I prayed, "Lord, help me to know what to say and how to say it." I claim Luke 12:12: "For the Holy Ghost shall teach you in the same hour what ye ought to say." I prayed that prayer all afternoon driving home from Wichita. So, based on that, I had to believe God answered my prayer and that indeed I had shared with my church what the Lord wanted me to share. Knowing what I would be doing, the church would be praying harder for me. No, I did not call World Help or become concerned.

Needless to say, the last instructions were somber ones. Among other items, I had to have a document notarized that I would not hold World Help responsible in case of danger. No other mission-sponsoring organization had made such a requirement. I must say this: World Help is up front with you. They hold nothing back. I appreciate their openness and truthfulness. I realized the seriousness of the trip. I did not share my concern or fear with Jim. I was afraid he might say I could not go (even though he would not have a right to do that since he had spent a year in Vietnam). But then I would have had a theological dilemma. Would I obey my husband or the Lord? But even more important, I was fearful I might give in to the fear I had about the trip. Psalm 56:3 kept coming to my mind, "What time I am afraid, I will trust in thee."

The trip got off to a great start. Sitting beside me, flying from Los Angeles to Hong Kong, was a team member from Nashville, Tennessee. At that time, it seemed fairly certain that my husband and I would be moving from Dallas to Nashville. So I had plenty of time to learn all about my future home. Upon arrival in Hong Kong, we had our final orientation meeting. We were told many important things: Our rooms and phone lines could possibly be bugged. The Bibles from that moment on were "bread" and other materials "crumbs." We had to sign another document acknowledging that we knew if we were interrogated or tortured we would not hold World Help responsible; the signing had to be witnessed by our roommate. How we would carry out the mission was explained in detail. We would be going into Mainland China in groups of six to eight at a time. Then we would be entirely alone, each of us going to different checkpoints. We could not talk to another American or draw attention to ourselves in any way. We must be able to think quickly and act like we knew exactly what to do. If an incident should develop, World Help could not get involved. We all accepted that because the organization could not afford to jeopardize its mission. I left that meeting with fifteen minutes remaining before our first journey.

Returning to my hotel room, I was absolutely overcome with fear. I had never been so scared in my whole life. I kept saying to myself, "I cannot do this. I just cannot go through with this assignment." I was absolutely overwhelmed with fear. But then, shear determination took over. I claimed Philippians 4:13: "I can do all things through Christ which strengtheneth me." It was his will that I come to China and he would see me through. Case closed. With that Scripture I exited the hotel not knowing what awaited me.

As a group, we walked from our hotel one-half mile to the subway. The heat was indescribable. I am not one ever to be bothered by heat, but the humidity in Hong Kong was extremely high. The first night my roommate and I thought our sheets were wet. They actually were dry; they just felt wet. Hosiery did not even dry overnight. When we got off the subway we walked another one-half mile to the location where the Bibles were stored. We each filled up a large duffle bag, wrapping clothes around the Bibles to further conceal them. Then we walked one-half mile back to the subway, carrying the extremely heavy bags, twenty-five to thirty pounds each, boarded the subway, and rode to the end of the line. We crossed the river bridge (Bay of South China Sea) and into Mainland Communist China. As we proceeded through many checkpoints, I would glance at the other five to six Americans; we were staggered twenty-five to thirty minutes apart. Many looked as white as a sheet. We were all praying for each other as we carried out our mission for the Lord.

The moment of reckoning came at the last checkpoint, which was the scanner. My Bibles were detected. Officials grabbed my bag and took me into a room. They started yelling at me, shaking their fists at me, and mumbling to one another. I had no idea what they were saying to me. There were no interpreters present. I did remember we were supposed to give up as few Bibles as we could, and even that if we only got one across the border, it would be a victory. So I shrugged my shoulders, playing dumb, and held up one finger, praying they knew I was asking permission to take one Bible. They screamed some more and shook their heads. I held up two and then three fingers but to no avail. I knew I had held off as long as I could, and I praised the Lord for boldness, but I was absolutely terrified.

I remembered I had my military identification card in my possession since Jim is a retired army lieutenant colonel. I did not want the authorities to know that. I had traveled with the card so I could receive medical care in Seoul from American doctors had there been a need. Thankfully, they did not ask for my purse. However, they asked for my passport. Folks, you have not lived until you turn your passport over to a communist authority in a communist country. I felt my life pass before me.

At the moment the passport left my hand, not a second before, 2 Timothy 1:7, "For God hath not given us the spirit of fear; but of power, and of love, and of a sound mind," became real and dear to me. It pays to memorize Scripture. I had an inner peace I cannot describe. I was no longer afraid. I had confidence everything was going to be all right. I was absolutely calm. I was experiencing a miracle! That was indeed one of the most precious moments of my life. I know I will never forget it. The Bill Gaither Chorus, "Whatever it takes to draw closer, I'm willing to do," took on a new meaning. Regardless of my fear after the orientation meeting or the absolute terror of the interrogation, it was worth it all to experience God's abiding presence at the moment of my deepest need. Later that week, I read in my devotional book, "God's rescue is never early, but never late." How applicable to my experience. I was reminded the safest place we can be is in God's will. Every child of God striving to be in his will is immortal until his work is finished.

The authorities copied down every detail of my passport. (I have told people that is why we live in Nashville now. If the

Chinese want to look for me, I no longer reside at the Dallas address on my passport.) The whole ordeal took about twenty minutes. It seemed an eternity to me. When they returned the passport to me and dismissed me, I looked around to see another team member. Misery loves company, you know.

Only three people got their Bibles in that day, but an exciting thing happened. There was an elderly couple on our team. They realized after that first trip across the border they could not physically make any more trips. I believe the Lord protected their Bibles so they would experience the thrill of delivering them to the Chinese pastors waiting outside the customs building. They accepted the Bibles with tears in their eyes. That was when we realized the whole mission trip was worth it. I met one Chinese pastor who had hand copied a Bible (it took him six months) just so he could have one. Do we cherish God's word that much?

What happens to the Bibles that are confiscated? The organization that assists World Help in China goes in the next day and purchases them. Your imagination reveals that God is mightily at work. The only way any Bible goes in is that God answers our prayers and closes the eyes of the scanner operators. It is amazing how easily they are distracted. New Chinese Christians are taking jobs as operators. During the entire mission trip, we got twenty-five hundred Bibles into Mainland China. To God be the glory!

We traveled by train to Guangzhou to attend Pastor Lamb's church. It was a house church with approximately six hundred square feet on three floors. About three hundred people began arriving three hours early; they sat on benches, the stairwell, and the floor, in stifling heat (one American fainted). They experienced constant harassment from the authorities. Their sound equipment was confiscated several months before we came. Such equipment was a priority because Pastor Lamb preached on the first floor, and his sermon was shown on closed-circuit TV on the other floors. All Bibles and hymnbooks were taken on one occasion. That has happened again since I returned. I heard about it on a Christian radio station.

Pastor Lamb's church is a highly visible church. Billy Graham has preached there, and Pastor Lamb has been to the United States.

He spent twenty years in prison for preaching the gospel. There were four hundred in church at the time persecution began. There are sixteen hundred now. He preaches the same sermon Sunday morning, evening, and Tuesday evening. They have to tell people for whom there is no room to return home. I wonder what it would be like to have to tell people to stay away from our services? They come twenty minutes before worship to pray, and the services last two hours. There are no chairs, only benches. What a humbling experience to sit in Pastor Lamb's presence and talk informally with him as we had opportunity after the service. Again, icing on the cake!

From Guangzhou, we flew three thousand miles to Beijing. This was the beginning of a new experience for me. For one who travels with two suitcases, I was asked to do the impossible! Use one tote bag for one week. Can you imagine such a thing? So cosmetics and everything went into one carry-on bag. Flexibility is the name of the game, right? Do not tell Jim I succeeded in this nonsense. Our favorite remark on the trip became, "I left it in Hong Kong." We decided when we got home and misplaced something that we would automatically say, "We left it in Hong Kong." There was a reason for this lack of luggage that I will share later.

Earlier, I reported on Aeroflot, the Russian airline. The Lord continues to "stretch" me. (Now I wonder if all these hair-raising experiences have happened to me to make exciting reading for you.) Remember the seat-belt scenario in Russia? There is a better scene than that. China Airways provides the opportunity to move from your seat with plenty of room. You just tip the seat in front of you much like you would exiting a back seat of a two-door car. The seats are not attached to the floor. Real comforting, huh? But we had good insurance—World Help agrees to get your remains back to the United States. That fact is not guaranteed on many mission trips. In fact, during orientation for Brazil, we were told to inform our families that Brazil will not allow for one's remains to be returned. World Help even has an arrangement whereby if one becomes seriously ill in China, a Chinese doctor in the States is notified. He instructs the doctors in China how to proceed. That was certainly reassuring.

A panoramic view of Tianamen Square in Beijing

Beijing was much cooler than Hong Kong, which makes it easier for the eight million bicyclists there. We enjoyed touring the Forbidden City, Summer Place, and Tianamen Square. We went through the cloisonne factory, and then came to the Great Wall! Yes, you guessed it. We climbed the Great Wall. Would I do less? There were 252 steps in Russia and 275 steps in Poland. I must not break my record. These, however, are not just any steps. Many are about a foot high. The handrails are low, so you have to bend way down to hold them, but there is reward for your endeavor.

I bought Jim a T-shirt stating, "I climbed the Great Wall." I wanted to cross out the I and put "My wife." For him to claim my feat would be heresy! This side trip was not all pleasure. We took in "bread and crumbs," delivering them to two Chinese pastors in

Certificate and photo of Jeannine Carter verifying that she climbed the Great Wall of China on May 22, 1995

Photograph of Great Wall—printed on back side of certificate verifying that Jeannine Carter climbed the wall on May 22, 1995

The Great Wall at Badaling

Beijing. Flying China Airways is never a problem; their scanners are not efficient enough to identify Bibles.

We flew back to Guangzhou and then to Hunan Island. I waded in the China Sea. I did not think a swimsuit was a necessary item in my tote bag for that week. After our day at the beach, we boarded a very full bus to Haiko. The buses there have a pull-down seat so the aisle is occupied also. No air-conditioning and people smoking made for a long eleven-hour ride, not to mention the mosquitoes swarming everywhere. Usually, if a mosquito is within one hundred miles, it finds me. I had not been taking malaria tablets either so I was very apprehensive. I only got six bites—another miracle! Also, since our knees were jammed up against the seat in front of us and our tote bags were on our laps, we understood why we were only allowed one bag. Can you envision a full-size suitcase on a lap for eleven hours? Praise the Lord for preliminary trips by organizations so that these "little" inconveniences are revealed.

In Haiko we visited a school. Afterwards, we boarded a school bus, rode into the country, and threw tracts out of the window at the peasants. As we threw them out, we would yell *Nhao* (pronounced knew-how) which meant "Hello, how are you?" We chuckled all the way. That was certainly a method of witnessing we had never tried. Believe it or not, most of the peasants stopped to retrieve the "crumbs," and many stopped to read the tracts.

Our final day in Hong Kong took us to Hong Kong Island to shop and tour on a double-decker bus. We had dinner and sharing time with the Americans who lived there permanently and had been our link to getting the "bread and crumbs" into Mainland China. We had been just the right size group. The previous year, sixty Americans had come, and the Chinese pastors told World Help never to bring that many again. They took in fifteen thousand pieces of "bread and crumbs." The pastors could not assimilate that much at one time. They had no place to store the materials. If they were caught with them, they could be sent to prison. We must be cognizant of the risk they live with daily. They thanked us for being an obedient group.

At the orientation meeting, we were told we must not hand out any religious tracts. Another group had come over six months before us and disregarded the rules. To this day, they probably do not realize that several Chinese pastors were imprisoned due to their lack of obedience. Again, it is so imperative to follow the guidelines of the coordinator. We succeeded in getting in twenty-five hundred pieces. To God be the glory!

Another telephone miracle occurred here. We were told to expect the lines to be tapped and to make no mention of our tasks. I thought, "Oh, no, Jim will probably ask, 'Did you get the Bibles in?'" So I planned to remedy that answer by replying, "That's classified." With our military background, he would know that meant I could not talk. Fortunately, the Lord took care of the most minute details. From observing the schedule, I had surmised the optional trip to Beijing was at the beginning of the trip. I had made much of that before I left. I like the side trips at the end so you can rest and relax before returning home. It was actually in the middle. So that allowed me to call Jim from Beijing. His conversation went something like this, "You haven't even started your real work, have you? You've just been having fun." Praise the Lord. He never even mentioned Bibles. Little did he know what experiences had already been mine.

Speaking of conversation, we don't realize the freedom we have in our country! One of our group, upon entering a somewhat nicer hotel than we had known previously, erupted with "Praise the Lord." One of the American residents there rushed to her and put a finger on her lips to remind her we must not make such a remark. When we met with the Chinese pastors in a hotel room, the television was turned up and they literally whispered to us. We take so much for granted in our nation. May God continue to bless America and may we ever have the privilege of speaking God's name throughout our land. "For unto whomever much is given, of him shall much be required" (Luke 12:48).

As many as twenty thousand people per day in China were becoming Christians in the early 1980s. Although seven million conversions a year seem to be astronomical growth, the number is not that impressive when compared to China's population of 1.1 billion. At that rate, it would take 150 years for all of China to become Christian. So the urgency to get Bibles in takes on new meaning, especially when one learns that ten Chinese come to Christ for each Bible distributed and that each Bible reaches three hundred lives (Ken Anderson, *Bold as a Lamb*, 157). God has allowed us to have the freedom. What will we do with it?

16

Responding to New Opportunities

Sweden 1996

W HEN I RETURNED FROM CHINA, I FELT THAT WAS my last mission trip. Why? The Lord had really impressed on me the need to write this book. China would be the fitting climax to the book. As I wrote in chapter 5, mission trips just get in your blood. I was drawn toward Cuba as I received 1996 material from World Help. I had to admit I was afraid. It was one thing to commit to China when I did not know what awaited me, but now I know the perils of Christian work in communist countries. I facetiously prayed, "Lord, I don't want a better climax to the book." But I have felt an inner peace. The trip had to be postponed due to our government's canceling all chartered flights from the United States to Cuba.

Again, God closes some doors and opens others. As this book goes to press, I have just returned from Sweden on a partnership mission trip with the Foreign Mission Board of the Southern Baptist Convention.

This trip represented a call for American Christians to commit to serve as volunteer missionaries. Because only ninety American Christians traveled to Sweden when Southern Baptists pleaded for 150 to go, four Swedish churches did not have mission teams. The Swedish pastor with whom I worked remarked, "The Foreign

Mission Board underestimated the enthusiasm of the Swedish Baptists for revival." Sadly, I had to explain the lack of enthusiasm on the part of local church members for traveling to Sweden even though the Foreign Mission Board had publicized the mission opportunity widely.

May all of us commit at this moment to be available the next time the Lord speaks to our hearts. Missions needs volunteers.

Conclusion

I N MANY RESPECTS I AM SAD TO BE CONCLUDING THIS book. Writing it has been an exciting experience. It is always fulfilling to be in the center of God's will. Since I had no plans to write a book, I confess I have not maintained detailed journals of my trips, but I have prayed that I might recall those experiences the Lord needed others to read. I trust you have enjoyed sharing with me. I have written as if I were talking one on one with you.

Most of all, I pray the Lord has spoken to you. My desire would be for the Lord to call you to go on a crusade—for you to realize God will equip you for the task he gives you. That includes physical strength, spiritual strength, and financial strength. Perhaps you are willing to go but do not have the financial means. International Crusades will tell you they have never had anyone for whom money did not become available when that person sincerely felt the Lord leading him/her to go on a crusade, stepped out on faith, and made plans to go. Many individuals who cannot go for health or family responsibilities will gladly make it possible for others to go. Sometimes pride gets in the way of making our needs known.

You may not be able to go, but there is something you can do that is just as important or perhaps more important. *Pray*. One of my most faithful prayer partners is a post polio-syndrome victim who has to use a wheelchair. She prays faithfully for me in my preparations, my trips, and my talks afterward. I firmly believe she has a part in each soul won to Christ. As the Holy Spirit makes hearts receptive to the gospel, he uses persons who will say, "Here I am, send me." Will you be the next person he uses? Can you identify with the old gospel song, "Ready"?

> Ready to suffer grief or pain,
> Ready to stand the Test;
> Ready to stay at home and send others if he sees best.
>
> Ready to speak, ready to think,
> Ready with heart and brain;
> Ready to stand when he sees fit, ready to stand the strain.
>
> Ready to go, ready to stay,
> Ready my place to fill;
> Ready for service, lowly or great, ready to do his will.
>
> —A. C. Palmer

If that is your commitment, then I know your testimony will be as mine:

> The longer I serve him, the sweeter he grows,
> The more that I love him, more love he bestows;
> Each day is like heaven, my heart overflows,
> The longer I serve him, the sweeter he grows.
>
> —Bill Gaither, 1965
> *Used by permission*

Epilogue

My Personal Testimony

PERHAPS YOU WOULD TELL ME YOU HAVE NO REASON to go on a mission trip. You do not have anything to share. You do not have a relationship with Jesus Christ. You have never asked him to come into your heart and accepted him as your personal Savior. One result of mission trips in my life has been a keen awareness that our city is a mission field. It is ludicrous if I go across the ocean to share Christ and do not tell my next-door neighbor about him. Whole churches have been transformed by large groups of their congregations going on partnership mission trips. These experiences have revived their visitation programs and other ministries. Church members realize how easy it is to share their personal testimony and lead someone to Christ. The missionary prayer calendars come alive as you recognize missionaries with whom you have served on the field or countries in which you have served. I have used the following International Crusades pamphlet. My prayer is that you will study it carefully and go through the questions and make the most important decision you will ever make: Where will you spend eternity?

My name is Jeannine Carter. I am from Nashville, Tennessee, USA. I am employed as a substitute teacher in the Nashville public schools and Christian schools in the city. I consider it a privilege to be in your country to share what Jesus Christ means to me.

As a nine-year-old child, I realized that Jesus Christ had come into the world and died that I might have eternal life. I knew that if I did not accept him as my personal Savior, I would never be able to go to heaven when I die.

Accepting Christ into one's heart should be just a beginning. The relationship should involve a lifetime commitment. As a mother of two boys and as an army officer's wife for twenty years, I have faced many crises in my life, including a year of geographical separation while my husband served in Vietnam. I found the Lord sufficient to meet all of my needs during those times.

I have seen the Lord work many miracles in my life. Examples of these miracles include earning a two-year master's degree in fourteen months and purchasing a home with a loan for 7 3/4 percent interest instead of the current 18 or 19 percent interest at that time. All of these events have shown me that God knows our needs and provides guidance in our everyday lives if we submit to him.

Let me urge you to confess your sins and accept Jesus as your personal Savior. Begin a lifetime commitment of walking daily with him. Know the Lord, and have the assurance of inner peace in this world and in death.

GOD'S PLAN FOR YOUR SALVATION

1. Do you believe in God? Yes No
2. Do you believe that God loves you? (John 3:16) Yes No
3. Do you believe that Jesus Christ is the Son of God? (Mark 1:1; 1 John 4:10) Yes No
4. Do you believe you are a sinner? (Rom. 3:23) Yes No
5. Do you believe that Jesus Christ died for your sins? (Rom. 5:8; 1 Tim. 1:15) Yes No

6. Do you want Jesus Christ to save you from your sins? (Rom. 6:23) Yes No

7. The Bible says, "That if thou shalt confess with thy mouth the Lord Jesus and shalt believe in thine heart that God hath raised him from the dead, thou shalt be saved." The Scripture also says, "For whosoever shall call upon the name of the Lord shall be saved." (Rom. 10:9, 13). Do you believe this? Yes No

8. Is there something keeping you from accepting Christ now? Yes No

9. You can receive Jesus Christ through faith expressed in prayer. Prayer is talking with God. Please read the following prayer and determine if this is what you want to ask God: "Dear Lord, I know I have done wrong and need forgiveness. Thank you for dying for my sins and for offering me eternal life. Please forgive my sins and help me turn from them. I now confess you as my Lord and receive you in my heart as my Savior. Take control of my life and make it full and meaningful. In Jesus' name, Amen." Does this prayer express what you want to ask God? Yes No

10. Do you want to pray right now and ask God to save you? Yes No

11. After praying, do you believe that Jesus Christ has come into your heart and saved you from your sins? (John 1:12) Yes No

BAPTISTS

We believe that all have sinned and that we need a Redeemer, and this Redeemer is the Lord Jesus, who died on the cross of Calvary in our place. Christ gives us *new life* when we accept him by faith, because we are not able to buy this salvation at any price.

Christ loves all people the same way: rich and poor, wise and ignorant, men and women, children, youth, and older adults.

And Christ, above all, loves *you*. He is searching for you and you need him. For this reason we invite you to come and listen to the eternal message of the Bible, the word of God.

Appendixes

Appendix I

Organizations That Sponsor Volunteer Mission Trips

International Crusades
500 South Ervay, Suite 409
Dallas, Texas 75201
214-747-1444

Campus Crusade for Christ
100 Sunport Lane, Department 3600
Orlando, Florida 32809
407-826-2680
Attn: International School Project. (Ask to go under the auspices of Association of Christian Schools International.) This is for convocations in the former Soviet Union.

Michael Gott Ministries
P. O. Box 2107
Jacksonville, Texas 75766
903-385-7657

World Help
P. O. Box 501
Forest, Virginia 24551
804-525-4657

Foreign Mission Board of the Southern Baptist Convention
P. O. Box 6767
Richmond, Virginia 23230
804-353-6655

Appendix II

Miscellaneous Items To Take

- Syringes (If you were to get sick in some countries, you would not want to be given an injection with their syringes. They use them repeatedly.)
- Puppets (These are handy when opportunities arise to work with children—kindergarten, mission groups, Sunday Schools.)
- Hymnals (These will help if you are called on to sing or play the piano.)
- Address labels (These prevent you from having to write your address numerous times upon departure. Add USA to address.)
- Wipes
- Alarm clock
- Calculator (Use it to figure money conversion—if you are as weak in math as I am.)
- Note paper
- Knife, spoon, fork (Some countries do not use silverware—India, hands; Japan and China, chopsticks. A spoon is convenient if you must take medicine and the knife to spread peanut butter.)
- Snacks (Peanut butter and instant oatmeal spared me from eating cucumbers for breakfast in Russia.)
- Insect repellent

- Flashlight (One came in handy when I had to walk down a long, dark hall in Romania to go to a toilet.)
- A bathroom cleanser
- Rubber bands
- Gum (Children everywhere expect gum.)
- Pedometer (Take one if you want to know how far you walk. I might have thought I walked one hundred miles in China if I had not had proof I walked only thirty-five miles.)
- Eye covers (These help keep light out if you are attempting to sleep on overnight flights.)
- Towel and wash cloth (In Russia we used hand towels for bath towels.)
- Scissors
- A disinfectant for skin abrasions
- Antibiotics (It is recommended to take Septra two times a day for preventive measures. It keeps your resistance up. I know there are two schools of thought on this subject. Some physicians say you must never take an antibiotic unless you are ill. But many physicians do not realize you do not always eat at safe American tourist spots. It is personal, but I prefer to follow the advice of organizations rather than a doctor who has not experienced the delicacies I have "enjoyed.")
- Water purifier (Brazil, Mexico, and India all have bottled water. Some places in Russia are getting bottled water. I always carry a purifier made strictly for international travel, not just one for camping in the United States; It is a PUR brand. Mine was purchased in California but the address on box is: Recovery Engineering, Inc., 2229 Edgewood Ave. South, Minneapolis, MN 55426. Take a container in which to carry water during the day.)
- Water purification tablets (Use these when you go into homes. In some countries, it takes twenty minutes of boiling to purify the water, so these tablets are helpful. However, they are very difficult to locate. I purchased mine at an army-navy store—I pass them off as saccharine if I get caught using them.)
- Luggage (I carry two pieces of luggage. I pack half and half. For instance, half of my shoes go in one, and half in the other.

Generally, you would not lose both pieces. Just do not lose yours in India. You cannot purchase a western-style dress, at least not in Hyderabad. A pastor's wife lost hers, and it was never located. She had to wear a sari the entire two weeks.)
- Pictures of your family and church (I usually do not show pictures of my house because even an unassuming house in the United States would appear to be a castle in many countries.)
- Adapter and transformer for curling irons and blow-dryers
- More film than you plan to use (Film is very expensive and sometimes nonexistent in many countries.)
- Passport (Be sure to check your passport expiration date—in case the country has a six-month requirement. Do not store an expired passport with your current one. One person arrived at the airport with an expired one and missed our plane. What an embarrassment!)

Appendix III

Theme Songs for the Crusades

Theme songs for the crusades have become much more meaningful to me. I can never sing one now without a flood of wonderful memories. They remind me to breathe a prayer for those involved in those crusades. Gene Lake (coordinator) admonished us in South Africa never to forget to pray for our new friends, new converts, and the churches. The churches have such an awesome responsibility to follow up after we leave. First Samuel 12:23 says: "God forbid that I should sin against the Lord in ceasing to pray for you."

Brazil—"Great Is Thy Faithfulness"
Rome—"Victory in Jesus"
South Africa—"Victory in Jesus"
Australia—"People Need the Lord"
Russia—"How Great Thou Art" (has fifteen verses in Russian)
Poland—"Love in Any Language"
China—"Revive Us Again" (sung informally by the Americans for physical revitalization amidst the intense heat and humidity)

Appendix IV

Shopping Suggestions

Many of you will want to know what would be good to shop for in some countries. There are excellent bargains many times. (And does not the Lord expect us to be good stewards of our money?) You wives may choose to tear this page out before your husbands read it. The treasures I have brought home remind me to pray for those countries. Many are conversation pieces in our home. It is usually best to seek advice from a national. Interpreters are a good source. American missionaries usually know the values. Be very discreet. It is usually wise not to take your interpreter shopping or to discuss prices. When you realize the average schoolteacher in Russia makes thirty dollars a month, we are all "rich Americans."

Brazil—stones (I bought a topaz ring, set in 14K gold, for $27. It is appraised for $175 in the United States.)

Mexico—sapphire ring

Rome—leather gloves for fifteen dollars; venetian glass bracelet; tiny gondola (I try to select mementoes that are typical of the area. Venice is famous for its gondolas.)

South Africa—rice beads; sandstone statuette; buffalo purse

India—a sari (I wore one that was given to me each time I spoke about India; I also have a miniature broom typical of India.

Australia—hand-crochet purse made by the Aborigines; sweat-shirt with Koala bears on front; didjeridoo, a musical instrument; black opal ring

Japan—Japanese doll; tea service

Romania—black pottery vase; linen

Russia—nesting dolls; dancing doll

Poland—farming apparatus typical of primitive farm equipment; amber jewelry, a gift from students in English class

China—China doll; tea service

Another type of bargain in many countries—be sure to frequent hair salons. Manicures and pedicures are often only four to five dollars. Getting your hair done can be a real experience. For example, in Germany I had to lean over forward. In Romania, they used a bucket to wash my hair.

Appendix V

Gifts of Appreciation

You will want to take gifts for your interpreters, the people whose homes in which you stay, the pastor, and others with whom you develop a close relationship. Give only what you can afford. I have seen Americans give expensive pens and other costly items. Here are some suggestions:

Hand towels
Ballpoint pens
Magnets—nationals love anything typical of your state
Trivets
Bandannas—especially appropriate for Texans
Bible markers
Plaques—if nationals speak English (if not, a very short verse like "God is love" is good).
Key chains

Appendix VI

Invitation To Write the Author

I know the Lord had a purpose in leading me to write this book. After reading my personal testimony, perhaps you have accepted Christ for the very first time; OR, perhaps you are now ready to step out on faith and commit yourself to go on a partnership mission trip; OR, perhaps you have been privileged to participate in a mission trip and would like to tell me something about your own experiences. I would love to hear from you. You may write in care of my publisher, and they will forward your letter to me. They have been such a delight to work with.

PROVIDENCE HOUSE PUBLISHERS
238 Seaboard Lane • Franklin, Tennessee 37067